THE
CALL

Martin Flanagan

ETT IMPRINT

Exile Bay

The 3rd revised edition published by ETT Imprint, Exile Bay in 2024

First published by Allen & Unwin in 1998
Published by ETT Imprint in 2021. Revised edition 2022
First electronic edition ETT Imprint 2021

ETT Imprint
PO Box R1906
Royal Exchange NSW 1225
Australia

ISBN 978-1-923024-73-1 (pback)
ISBN 978-1-922473-63-9 (ebook)

Cover: Tom Wills (centre, back row) with members of the 1868 Aboriginal Cricket team

The author's end-piece was first published in an earlier form in *the Age* on September 26 2021

Design by Tom Thompson

Contents

Though riders be thrown in black disgrace,
Yet I mount for the race of my life with pride,
May I keep to the track, may I not fall back
And judge me, O Christ, as I ride my ride

12th century Irish prayer translated into English by Douglas Hyde

Author's note

This book is an imagining of real events. It does not purport to be a history; rather, it is an interpretation of an historical drama in the manner of a work for theatre or the screen. However, because it does rely on historical research, I have people to thank. First and foremost, I wish to thank those members of the Wills family who assisted me, particularly David Wills Cooke, who made available to me copies of the correspondence of many of the characters involved, and Zita, Roderick and Tom Wills of Minerva Creek station in Queensland for their extraordinary hospitality and the guided tour of the Springsure district, including the former Cullin-la-ringo station, which they gave me. No mention of the Wills family can be complete without mention of my former football teammate, David Spence, his mother Judy and cartoonist Kaz Cooke, all of whom encouraged me in this project at different times.

I would like to thank Melbourne historian, Rex Harcourt, for generously supplying me with a substantial body of research on Tom Wills. *Cricket Walkabout* which Rex co-authored with John Mulvaney, was also one of my sources. It is not my intention to supply a bibliography. My reading veered far and wide of the subject; on occasions, too far and too wide so that I became immersed in the mire beneath the hospitals in the Crimea or the pre-history of Melbourne. However, I do feel obliged to mention certain texts. R. V. Pockley's *The Edward Wills Family and Descendants in Australia* 1797-1976 is a commendably forthright family history, while *Running with the Ball,* the name given to H.C.A. Harrison's autobiography when it was re-published in 1987, with notes and additional text by Anne Mancini and Gillian Hibbins, can be relied upon for its scholarship. For people wishing to pursue the subject of the Cullin-la-ringo massacre, the most thorough account I came across was Lorna McDonald's *Rockhampton - A History of City & District.* The written instructions to the Port Phillip Native Police and Lieutenant Frederick Walker's testimony to the Queensland parliamentary inquiry into the Native Police are both public documents, but I wish to acknowledge that I came across them in Henry Reynold's book, *With the White People.* However, this is not to suggest that all the documents in the book are actual. Some are amalgams or re-workings of existing documents, some are inventions. Also, as indicated in the text, the idea that Johnny Mullagh's eminence in white culture may have been associated with a 19th century secessionist movement in the western districts of Victoria is not original. I first encountered it in an article on Mullagh by South Australian sports historian Dr Bernard Whimpress. I would like to thank my guide in Djabwurrung country, Neil

Murray, and my guide at Rugby school, the chief librarian in the William Temple Reading Room, Rusty MacLean. I would like to thank Peter Robertson for leading me to Johnny Mullagh's waterhole and local landowner David Edgar for opening his family papers on Mullagh to me. The list could go on, but I will end it there.

As always, I would like to thank my wife Polly for her courage and good sense. I would like to thank three friends who were never more than a phone call away, Paul Bateman, Kate Cahill and Dianne Lee, and a diviner of dreams, Marie Watt. I would also like to acknowledge my brother Richard's companionship along the creative path, Meredith Rose's incisive editing and the support and care of my original publisher, Sophie Cunningham, and her staff. Finally, I want to thank my dog Mo, who understands that words are footprints and padded along beside me, every step of the way.

Martin Flanagan Melbourne 1998

1
T.W.W.

The best way to start this story is by going to the ground. Get off the train at Richmond station and walk along Punt Road. Try and ignore the four lanes of pent-up toxic traffic, pass the charmless pub with the mirror windows and the sign advertising topless barmaids and strippers, then cross at the lights. Yarra Park awaits you. Climb the slope and pass through what I call the native garden-lemon-scented eucalypts, their creamy-grey trunks flushed with a hint of pink and purple, giant Tasmanian blue gums with shattered bark and liquid dancing leaves-but keep in mind that, really, this is red gum country. Red gums are my trees. Nothing to look at - dull, dirty-white trunks, tangled matted hair-but inside the colour of clotted blood. They bleed, believe you me. Yarra Park has three scarred red gums. The biggest is on the brow of the hill between Punt Road and the cricket ground. The wound in its side begins above my head and finishes at my feet. A piece of bark the shape and size of a door was tapped away and probably used to make a canoe. This is an old Wurundjeri camping ground, so I've read. First name after white settlement? Richmond paddock - the troopers kept their horses here.

I come here on days when I'm not at the library. I sit or stand beside the scarred tree, usually with a piece of paper in my hand, a newspaper clipping or an old diary entry, reading aloud. No-one asks me what I'm doing, which is probably just as well because I'm looking for someone who's not here. Tom Wills disappeared – 'the Grace of Colonial Cricket'. Imagine what English cricket would be like if it had mislaid the memory of its Grace. *What he lacked he would not need. All that he had he could use.* A black Trinidadian named C.L.R. James wrote that. He said that the Victorian age couldn't be understood without reference to three figures - W.G. Grace; Dr Thomas Arnold, the headmaster of Rugby school; and Thomas Hughes, the author of *Tom Brown's Schooldays*. Tommy's connected to all three. He arrived at Rugby only a few years after Arnold died of a heart attack, he returned to Victoria the year before Hughes's book hit Melbourne; and, eventually, as was his wish, he met Grace 'on the field of play'. Tommy's an ornament to the game, as we say in this country, but you won't find him in the trophy cabinet. I know, I've looked.

No-one in his day thought he was easily forgotten.

A mere seven days after landing at Queen Street pier in December 1856,

T.W.W., as he was then known, turned up at a trial match for the Victorian XI and was 'the most observed of the observed'. For his debut performance, wrote Alfred Bonicelli, 'Spectator' of the *Melbourne Illustrated News*, T.W. Wills chose the costume of the I Zingari club. I Zingari's colours of red, yellow and black, then largely unknown in the colony, gave vivid expression to the knightly cry, "From darkness, through fire, to the light!" He completed his outfit with two-tone shoes and a brocaded cap, while his complexion, pallid after six years in England, accentuated the fact that his brown whiskers were curled. The previous year, no less an authority than *Bell's Sporting Life* had declared him to be one of the most promising young cricketers in England. In those days hundreds, not to say thousands, would gather at the Melbourne Cricket Club's ground in the bush surrounds of the Richmond paddock for such a match, and when young Tommy stepped from the Melbourne club's weatherboard pavilion, a sway-backed youth on the boundary was heard to remark, 'Who's the flash cove?'

The first skill 'the flash cove' displayed was his swiftness in retrieving balls. He ran them down, turned and, in a single action, unleashed throws which barely left the line of the horizon as they flew to the keeper. Invited to bowl, he steadied himself ten or twelve paces from the wicket, lightly tossing the red orb in his fingers, his otherwise impassive features flushed. His approach to the wicket was deceptively sedate. Then, in the act of delivering the ball in the regulation round-arm manner, he gave a sudden heave. The ball was through the batsman's defence before he saw it, striking him a painful blow on the thigh; his involuntary cry was heard from the boundary. Wills returned to his mark without apology. All eyes and ears were upon him now. His next ball, delivered with the same action, was slow out of the hand. It hung mesmerisingly in the air before gripping and twisting upon meeting the pitch. The poor batsman was left swatting at the ball as if it were a. housefly. The third ball, delivered low and fast, shattered his stumps and returned him to the pavilion. No less a master than Alfred Mynns, the Lion of Kent, was said to have taught Tom Wills his craft, praising his fierce, proud spirit and affectionately calling him 'my lad'. If anything, T.W.W.'s batting aroused even greater comment. It was utterly without style. Indeed, there was some discussion in the members' pavilion as to whether it could properly be termed batting. True, what he hit he hit hard, but for the rest of the time he poked the ball through gaps in the field and ran like a gun dog between the wickets. However, while the debate in the pavilion was proceeding, he top-scored in both innings. 'He was then only 21 but his mastery of the field was evident for anyone with eyes to see.' Again Alfred Bonicelli, 'Spectator' of the *Melbourne Illustrated News*.

Far from being unremarked upon, Tom Wills's triumphant return to the colony was *news*. It fired the ambition that Victoria might vanquish New South Wales on the field of manly play, such a result being deeply desired. The parent colonies of New South Wales and Van Diemen's Land - recently renamed, - to no-one's confusion, Tasmania - represented a dark and shameful past from which the good people of Victoria were desperate to distance themselves. A pamphlet circulated in 1850, the year Tommy left for England, shows Victoria as an innocent maid waving away a convict transport anchored in Port Phillip Bay. Rumours that sodomy was endemic among the male convict population in Van Diemen's Land had been confirmed by the Superintendent for the District of Port Phillip, Charles La Trobe, after a visit he made to the island at the instruction of the Secretary of State for Colonies, William Gladstone. There were stories too of cannibalism among the convicts, who were also blamed for the atrocities committed against the natives during the island's Black War. The heart-shaped island with the impassable corner of wilderness in the southwest had acquired the stigma of a place in which nature was turned hopelessly and horribly upon itself.

By the time Tom Wills returned to Victoria, it was the wealthiest colony in the British Empire and in a position to indulge its pretensions. Melbourne's civic fathers, most notably an Irish judge named Sir Redmond Barry, had begun the business of transforming the settlement into a metropolis worthy of its status as an imperial prodigy. A statue of Sir Redmond is to be found outside the State Library of Victoria. I nod to him each day as I pass. How can I not? His library is my sanctuary. Outside its stone walls, oily voices parade their superficial concerns on radio and television, while newspapers shout to make themselves heard. Libraries are a chance to escape the madness. Remember William Buckley, the convict left behind when Colonel David Collins aborted his attempt to establish Hobart on the shores of Port Phillip Bay in 1803? Thirty-two years later, dressed in a possum-skin cloak and with a tongue that clacked about in his head like a digging stick, he walked into the camp of John Batman, so-called founder of Melbourne, on the other side of Port Phillip Bay. I came across a picture of Old Buck in an encyclopedia when I was a kid and knew him at a glance. Long-haired like a prophet, light of manly independence in his eye, white master of his new-found world-this was our Robinson Crusoe. Several decades later, in the State Library of Victoria, I found another picture of him, a pencil sketch from a notebook kept by J .H. Wedge, Batman's surveyor. Old Buck is sitting cross-legged in the dirt. Like a black. That's what I mean about libraries. At the end of each age, when the' tide of self-interest finally recedes, you can find out what was going on beneath the bright reflecting surface.

When I started reading about Tommy Wills and collecting bits and pieces about him, it was because I liked the things he did. He reminded me of kids I'd known at school the ones who thrilled me with their daring and made me laugh out loud. It took me a while to see that there was more to the story, that like W.G. Grace he was 'both himself and more than himself'. T.W. Wills was a sporting hero, possibly Victoria's first, and that's saying something. Victorian perhaps, more accurately, Melbourne - is a character in this story. When Sir Arthur Conan Doyle visited Melbourne in 1920 and cast his highly deductive eye about he likened it to Edinburgh, where he had grown up. Both cities were outposts of Empire which took their character from a soberly ambitious middle class. In fact, the continent as a whole impressed Sir Arthur. As far as the land was concerned, three words would describe it - gum, wattle and scrub-but he was impressed by its potential. He likened it to an engine of enormous horsepower which as yet did not have sufficient people to harness it, but he also perceived the dilemma confronting the young nation: how to increase population without diluting its British stock? His suggestion was that it seek to attract migrants from North America.

He did have two criticisms of Melbourne, however, and was forthright in making them: there were a disproportionate number of drunks on the streets, and the whole city - in fact, the whole nation! - stopped for a horse race, the Melbourne Cup, which Sir Arthur described as a lottery on legs. Neither fault need prove terminal, he wrote upon his return to England, because each could be remedied quickly enough through legislation. But Sir Arthur, we now know, was wrong. For more than six decades, Phar Lap, the horse that won the 1930 Melbourne Cup, stood in an illuminated glass case in the same building as the State Library of Victoria, surrounded by other objects of wonder, such as Egyptian crypts, dinosaur skeletons and minerals that glow in the dark. Sir Arthur was a man of singular vision. His mistake was to presume Melbourne had a single nature.

Sir Arthur attended the 1920 Victorian Football League grand final as a guest of the Melbourne Cricket Club. During the pre-match luncheon, he was seated at the head table beside a slim, impeccably mannered gentleman in his eighties. Colden Harrison was first introduced to Sir Arthur as the former Registrar-general of Titles for Victoria and then as the Father of Australian football. The two dignitaries found little to disagree about. After receiving his knighthood for championing Britain's militarist policies in South Africa during the Boer War, Sir Arthur had lost his eldest son in World War I. Only one of Colden Harrison's four sons had survived infancy and he had died at a young age; but Harrison's son-in-law had been killed in the. War. Both hoped the terrible sacrifice had been worth it and nodded in mute agreement about the treachery of the Catholic Archbishop of Melbourne, Irishman Daniel Mannix, who had led the campaign which defeated the Australian government's plan to introduce conscription after the British Army suppressed the 1916 Easter Uprising in Dublin.

When the luncheon ended, Harrison invited Sir Arthur to accompany him to the balcony, where they were seated and offered travelling rugs to put over their legs. By then, the large stadium was rumbling with the sound of sixty thousand expectant people. Nothing in what Sir Arthur subsequently wrote suggests Tom Wills's name arose in the course of the afternoon, yet Colden Harrison was Tom Wills's cousin. His wife, Emily, was Wills's sister. Sir Arthur's generally favourable observations of Australian football are to be found in his book, *Wanderings of a Spiritualist.* From the point of view of spectacle, he thought it the best code of football he had seen, the comparisons he had in mind being with rugby and soccer. This would have pleased Colden Harrison, who actively promoted the belief that Australian football was a British game, but it is clear that, notwithstanding the fact that he possessed a famously inquiring mind, no-one directed Sir Arthur's attention to the writings of James Dawson, a Scottish selector who lived in the western districts of Victoria during the early years of white settlement. Dawson witnessed an Aboriginal game which he called football being played at *korroboreas,* or meetings of the clans, one of which he identified as the *chappwurrung,* otherwise spelt Djabwurrung. Tom Wills spent his childhood among the Djabwurrung, speaking their language. When he was fifteen, he left for Rugby. This is his first letter, or the first that I have found. Dated London, August 1850:

My   Dear   Father,
I am glad to inform you that we all arrived in good health after a very tedious passage of five months. We called in at Simons town at the Cape of Goodhope for some provisions and we took in another passenger at St Helene's. We had four very stormy nights and the last one carried away our Flying Gibboom. I saw more vessels in one day at the mouth of the Thames than I ever did at Port Phillip in twelve months. Captain Dalgarno *[The C in Captain is written with a flourish which makes it larger than any other capital on the page]* taught me the way to splice and also to map make knots and to take the sun. We passed every vessel that we saw while the wind blew for we very seldom had a breeze that lasted above twelve hours at one time we thought that we should never get home, and we also feared that the provisions should run short. The Sea that the wind got up was so bad that they were obliged to burn biscuit and make it into coffee. *[Punctuation is*

random. Here and there, a sentence begins before its predecessor has ended. Characteristic errors.]

I hope that you all arrived safe at 'Lexington' after I left you and that you have got the better of your cough. I have only wrote these few lines to let you know that I am arrived safe as I know that you will be very anxious for me and I am glad to say that there is another ship to Port Phillip in a few days and I shall give you a long description of the voyage

I remain
Your Son
T.W. Wills

The script? Large and featureless. Without style, unless filial duty can be termed a style. Young Tommy clearly saw letter writing as an act of labour, something that had to be done, like building fences. The letter is addressed, significantly, to his father. In the archives of the Victorian Cricket Association is an unfinished handwritten manuscript which attempts to intertwine Tom Wills's life and that of his father and present them as having a common theme. It has three beginnings *and no end.* That is a clue in itself. The title? Something rousing to the ear - 'Blazing Trails Sporting and Pastoral.' Date? Circa 1920 - that is, the aftermath of World War I. About the time Sir Arthur visited Melbourne. Author unknown, but clearly an enthusiastic amateur. Here is the first start to:

'Blazing Trails Sporting and Pastoral'

Horatio Wills left Molonglo Plains, near what is now called Canberra, with his wife and infant son (young Thomas being then just three years old) in August 1838 and set off in the footsteps of Major Thomas Mitchell who had named the magnificent country he had traversed three years earlier to the south Australia Felix. What a privilege was Mitchell's, to examine and open to Britain a country to hold millions of her people! In the covered wagons of the day, Wills senior left Sydney with a band of twenty men who were to exercise vigilance against wandering aboriginal tribes. Early in 1839, Mr Wills selected a homestead site in the vicinity of a mountain named by him Ararat because 'here, like the Bible, we rested'. On this site, he built his grand house 'Lexington' which still stands-very weatherworn, but habitable - to this day!

As kangaroos, emus, fish and food of all kinds were plentiful in these parts it was natural that the Aboriginal tribes should be in strong force in the Vicinity. These dusky native owners of the country were by no means backward in indicating to the newcomers that their uninvited occupancy of their lands should be adequately paid for and, as a consequence of this belief, goods of all kinds made mysterious disappearances. Wills was naturally humane and, assisted by his wife, he quickly made friends with the local tribes by means of amicable overtures to the visiting lubras and their pick-aback piccaninnies. A tactical advance for friendship with the natives was also made by Wills who postured daily to the Sun and Moon, such performances being viewed with awe! Amity was further secured by the queen of the local tribe claiming the squatter as her son for, it was evident to her mind, that he must be a 'jump-up blackfellow', like the long-escaped convict William Buckley as did he not have the same deep scar around his ankle that her dead son possessed when he was in the flesh?!

Thus gifts of good food and flour, a sympathetic womanly heart, and uniform kind but firm treatment by the master brought about a mutual feeling of goodwill and trust enabling the onerous work of the run to progress with satisfaction to all. Young Tom Wills soon became another link in the chain of affection between white and black for he was the idol of the girls and the playmate of the picaninnies. Playing the games and singing the songs of the younger gnomes of the forest, little Tommy steadily imbibed the language and learnt the tricks and forest lore of his wonderful playmates. Even so, who would have dreamt that in manhood's prime he would lead a band of his playmates of the forest to green cricket swards where they would defeat on level terms a representative team of players from the conquering white race in the presence of Royalty?!

Wrong. The match - the Aboriginal team's last before leaving for England - was played at the Albert Ground in Sydney in February 1868 and watched by Prince Alfred, the Duke of Edinburgh, then making the first visit to Australia by a member of the British Royal Family, in the course of which he would be shot and wounded by an Irishman named O'Farrell during a picnic on the Sydney Harbour foreshore. But Tom Wills didn't play. Nor did he go on the tour of England later that year, despite being at the height of his powers. 'Take him all in all, the Captain of the Victorian Eleven is the best cricketer in Australia.' He wanted to go. William Tennant, 'Fine Leg' of the *Australasian,* was at a loss to understand why Wills's feelings were 'so injured at his exclusion'.

In seeking to understand the fate which befell the son, it is necessary to trace the trajectory of the father. A portrait of Horatio Wills shows a short, stout man with florid cheeks and small eyes that suggest a shrewd, busy intelligence. 'If phrenology be a true science, I have high hopes for my son!' That's Horatio's voice. His diaries, addressed to Tom and begun when the boy was seven, can be found in the State Library of Victoria, along with the letters subsequently written by his son in the course of his many disputes with colonial cricket's governing bodies. 'Divinity doth shape our ends/ Rough-hew them as we may.' This quote, borrowed from Hamlet, the young Prince of the Danes, appears a number of times in Tommy's correspondence, usually letters of resignation, of which over the years he wrote more than his share. Horatio reserved his attempts at eloquence for his diaries. In his speech he was plain and blunt, like the seaman he had once, been.

In the family history, Horatio Wills is the First Man. The first man to import a wool press into Australia (a massive wooden structure 18 feet high with a steel windlass it took two men to operate, which he later dragged on the back of a dray to Queensland). The first man to import barbed wire to keep dingoes from his sheep. The first man to import strychnine for use as a bait when the fences proved ineffective. Painfully aware of his own lack of education, he sent Tom to Rugby, then entering its period of greatest eminence, and despatched his second and third sons, Cedric and Horace, to school in Germany, one to learn about wool growing - Horatio admired the merino flocks of Saxony - the other to become a vigneron because he foresaw that Australia would have a wine industry. The list of Horatio Wills's achievements culminates in him donning a pith helmet at the age of 50 and setting out once more for the frontier, notwithstanding the fact that it was now 1000 miles to the north in the newly created colony of Queensland. Four short, abrupt hills at the end of a gravelly plain 200 miles inland from Rockhampton - Mount Horatio, Mount Spencer, Mount Howe, Mount Wills - bear testament to the first man's enduring power.

Tom Wills had his father's red cheeks and, later, his balding head, but at five feet ten inches (*Lilywhite's Cricket Biographies*) was the taller by three inches. 'When in cricket costume, few athletes boast a more muscular form.' Were they Churchills? For the best part of a century, their descendants thought so, believing Horatio's father, Edward Wills, to be the illegitimate son of the fourth Duke of Marlborough, George Spencer. Both could certainly behave in a Churchillian manner. 'As a commander in the field, T.W.W. is without equal' (and that was written by one of his most hostile critics, J.B. Ellis of the *Argus*). Twenty years earlier, when foot-pads arrived to stick up 'Lexington', Horatio invited them in for breakfast. One of their number growled that he had come for booty, not breakfast, whereupon Horatio turned to the gang leader and said, 'You are in command here, Sir, are you not?' and the man ordered his surly companion to hold his tongue. Or so the story goes. The life of the father - unlike that of the son - was to receive many posthumous decorations. In *An Australian Pioneer*, written by Horatio's granddaughter Agatha Wills Booth in 1911 to commemorate the centenary of his birth, Horatio Wills is likened to Abraham, the great patriarch of the Old Testament. This is Agatha Wills Booth's account of Abraham's native youth. Observe his winning ways:

We who have lived to enjoy the benefits of this new country do not, I fear, fully appreciate the hardships and privations endured by those who brought our good fortune about. Such a man was my grandfather, Horatio Spencer Wills, who was the son of Edward Spencer Wills, a Sydney merchant who came to Australia as a young man from London to try his luck in a new land. Although Horatio's mother later re-married Robert Howe, sometimes called 'the Father of the Press in New South Wales', my grandfather possessed an adventurous nature and, at an early age, ran away to sea. Six months later, his poor mother was informed that the vessel upon which her last-born had sailed had been wrecked in the Pacific Ocean with the loss of all on board. With the passage of time and much sadness, my grandfather's family gave him up for dead. Imagine, then, the excitement and jubilation when, two years later, a young man with her son's blue eyes and mischievous grin was seen striding through the streets of Sydney with long flowing hair, darkened skin and a South Sea Island spear in his hand.

Through his quick wit and courage, Horatio had survived! His boat had indeed been wrecked on a coral island, only three of the crew making it to shore. Savages had then fallen upon them, clubbing his two compatriots to death. This fate would also have befallen my grandfather had he not spied a girl of about thirteen years standing beside an old man watching the terrible spectacle. Instead of waiting for an axe to descend upon him, my grandfather ran and threw himself at the girl's feet, grabbing her hands and begging for her protection little knowing that she was the princess of the island and that the stern-faced man beside her was her father, the chief. So moved was the princess by the handsome young man's entreaties, he was spared, and such was the winning effect of my grandfather's personality that, within a short time, the Chief came to see him as a match for his daughter in marriage.

And so, for two years, Horatio Wills lived among savages, observing their ways and sharing their food; but he always planned to escape and, eventually, when a trading vessel stopped at the island and sent a boat ashore for water, he saw his opportunity. Taking a moment when his guards were otherwise occupied, he dived from a tall cliff into the broil-

broiling waters of the ocean. The moment he came to the surface, spears fell about him. Canoes were manned and launched, and it quickly became a race for life and death. When the sailors in the boat realized it was a white man thrashing towards them, they rowed like men 'possessed' to pick him up. Those on board the ship hastily made ready to raise the row-boat the moment it reached them while others of the crew ran for arms. With the natives hurling their spears at close quarters, the ship got underway and my Grandfather gave thanks to God the Almighty that he had been saved from. a life among savages and was returning to his loved ones. The Island upon which he had been tossed is one of the Marquesas group which lies mid-way between Australia and South America, some miles north of the Pitcairn Island made famous by the crew of the Bounty.

What about Tommy's mother - what sort of person was she? In 1841, when George Augustus Robinson, the Protector of Aborigines in the District of Port Phillip, met her at 'Lexington', she was fraught and fearful. A companion portrait to that of her husband shows a woman with a long face and her son Tom's large pale eyes. In Horatio's diaries she is the object of his most fervent religious devotions, but as a person she appears only twice. Once she reminds Horatio of how, when they first arrived at 'Lexington', Tommy was left in the tent with his baby sister. The parents heard him screaming and ran back to find him terrified that the 'bullabees' were coming to take them away. 'His mother was much alarmed by his fear but I told her it was a young boy's foolish fancy.' Horatio also recalls that even as a toddler Master Tom liked a drink. He would approach his mother with a vial and ask for beer, saying, 'It been a long day.' 'The little guzzler is his mother's prototype.'

Elizabeth Wills was born Elizabeth McGuire in Dublin. After her death her maiden name was changed to Wyre. The forgery can be easily seen in a letter written by Horatio to his brother Thomas the week after the wedding. The neat, ordered script continues for several pages before disappearing into a grey smudge when the subject of the 16-year-old bride's name arises. Eventually, what emerges, grandiosely written, like a carriage from a grubby fog, is the surname Wyre. Principal suspect? Agatha Wills Booth, in whose possession the document was for many years. Why? Because whether or not Elizabeth McGuire from Dublin was Catholic, she sounded as if she was, and if there is one thing Abraham never does in any Creation Story it is marry out of the one true faith - in this case, Presbyterianism. For those who aspire to respectability, finding suitable clothing in which to dress up the past has long been part of what being Australian means.

In a past life I was a conductor on Melbourne's trams. I wasn't the wittiest conductor or the most charming, but I liked what I did and made enough money to purchase an old Ford Telstar with pseudo-velvet seats that sat like a lorry on the road. One Sunday, the Ford Telstar and I drove the fifty flat and dreary miles to Geelong, Victoria's second city, on the western side of Port Phillip Bay. Just past the town, jutting into the waters of the bay, is a spur of land called Point Henry. At the height of the Gold Rush, while Tom was still at Rugby, Horatio Wills sold 'Lexington' and brought his ever-expanding family here, even though it meant starting anew and living in a tent. The location, close to a major settlement without being part of it, smacks of marital compromise. Even now, it's half and half - a bird sanctuary bordering an industrial site. During his decade at Point Henry, Horatio Wills experimented furiously with soil improvement, mixing tons of shells he gathered from the local beaches with cartloads of offal he collected from the abattoir; traded in gold on a commission basis for a firm in London; was elected president of the local Agricultural Society; became an elder of the kirk-and got bored. 'My father would stand for hours in the paddock, looking to the north, hands clasping and unclasping behind his back.' (Emily Harrison, nee Wills.)

'Lexington' is a further 150 miles to the north-west, just south of Ararat. This is where Tom Wills spent his childhood, miles from any neighbour. The nearest town, Moyston, is an elbow-bend in a back road with a shop and a stone war memorial on one side, and a couple of square brick houses with silver roofs on the other. Half a mile down the road is a footy ground with the obligatory line of dark pines on the windward side of the oval. 'Called to see Horace Wills at "Lexington" and beheld the comic spectacle of his small boy released from prayer like an arrow from a bow running off to join his playfellows in the camp of the blacks.' (Captain Allison, a landowner in the area.) A mile or so away, up a long rise, is the first house Horatio built, the roof of its verandah pulled low like the brim of a tin hat. The weathered bricks are a fresh orange colour. Constructed in a square, the old house has a hollow interior for the protection of inmates during attacks. Horatio Wills opposed the establishment of a native reserve in the area, saying it would destroy the confidence of the sheep industry. He had gone to a lot of trouble to conciliate the local blacks, he told the Superintendent for the District of Port Phillip, Charles La Trobe, and a native reserve would attract 'wild tribes of predatory blacks'. He didn't add that most were probably starving.

The wire gate guarding the track into the property was locked the day I visited. Apart from a few old red gums with deep ritual cuts in their withered guts, the undulating paddocks were empty and bare. I had hoped to see a white cockatoo. As I understand it, Aboriginal people conceive of the universe roughly in the manner of yin and yang. The two in ancestral spirits this part of the continent are Grugidj and Gabadj, the white and black cockatoo, and all living creatures are governed by the duties and obligations arising from their relationship to them. An old map in the State Library suggested that the local clan when Horatio Wills arrived 'belonged' to Grugidj. What I saw was a hawk that dropped from a tree not a yard from my face, then slowly levered itself into flight, its broad speckled wings making a faint brushing sound in the hot air. Mount Ararat, named by Horatio, is a pimple to the east. The old house, with its thick glass eyes, looks towards the wild leaping profile of the mountains rising abruptly from the khaki plain 20 miles to the west. The area's Scottish pioneers named them the Grampians despite the fact they look nothing like the bald, velvet humps of their homeland with their gold and brown coverings. These have orange escarpments caught in the ad of breaking from the earth like furious brows. They have stone slopes that shine like old leather and dark, dank gulleys with eucalypts of enormous girth and secret caves. Tom Wills grew up in sight of the mountains where the Djabwurrung said fire first fell to earth, receiving daily instruction from his father in Arithmetic, Spelling and the New Testament. Then, following a brief spell at a private academy in Melbourne, during which time he received a black eye while playing his first game of cricket on the area of land now occupied by Spencer Street station, he arrived at Rugby, a colonial youth with no gift for speech but a certain fire in his soul.

Tom Brown's Schooldays, Chapter 5, 'The Fight'

> As it is our well-weighed intention to give a full, true and correct account of Tom's only single combat with a schoolfellow in the manner of our old friends Bell's Life, let those young persons whose stomachs are not strong, or who consider a good set-to with the weapons which God had given us all an uncivilized, unchristian, or ungentlemanly affair, just skip this chapter, for it won't be to their taste.

'Blazing Trails Sporting and Pastoral' - second start

> Tom Wills at 15 years of age had been sent to Rugby. Tall, athletic, learned in the lore of the bush and strong, he was not altogether innocent of the wiles of the students of the great schools of England. His arrival had been duly heralded, his future schoolmates having been informed that a 'chum' from the Australian colonies was about to join them. Enough said! Orders for the customary rag went forth.

Three burly students were to seize and strip him after supper and, after duly tossing him in a blanket, he was to be assigned his daily routine of duties as fag to his senior. Lights out at 10 pm saw the janitor turning his back on the students and giving the newcomer a muttered warning as he reached the doorway.

Tommy had been told of the fagging business before leaving Australia, but, nurtured in a stern bushman's school & blessed with a constitution of iron, he was not likely to kow-tow to any prig of quality who might wish to make a toady of him. The lad's activities with his black companions had been extremely useful also. The spear, nulla-nullas, woomeras and boomerangs were definite lethal instruments in his hands when at the chase with his faithful dusky cobbers.

A few minutes after 10 pm, a flare indicated the opening of the attack. On the command 'Up & at him lads!' a rush was made towards the victim. To the surprise of the room, he was found to be on-guard, a pronged spear in one hand and a boomerang in the other! At this apparition, the startled attackers gave pause & were greeted with an astonishing war-cry, at which a retreat was made in fear and trembling that bodily hurt might ensue and expulsions might result as a consequence of such a major disturbance. A truce was called, the weapons were put away and Tommy was thereafter left carefully to his own devices.

All lessons are in a single hall with high dark wooden walls into which generations of Rugby boys have carved their names and initials, the only sound the murmur of verse. In one term, the senior form, the VIth, are required to commit to memory the eleventh book of Virgil's *Aeneid* and the fourth book of his *Georgics;* the eleventh and twelfth satires of Juvenal; the fourth book of Lucretius, plus passages from the Bible. A report card shows that T.W. Wills topped his form, a group of 14, on at least one occasion. His best subject? Repetition - 880 marks. Phillips, 610, and Dangerfield, 420, were next, while poor old Ireland, on 44, couldn't remember a thing he was told. Punishment for talking during a lesson: six strokes of the cane (the headmaster alone uses the birch). Fewer expulsions than in Dr Arnold's day, when boys deemed to be of little moral worth, or 'character', were jettisoned on whatever pretext came to hand. Outside classes, the boys are basically left to their own devices.

Prefects, called praepostors, administer the cane across the shoulders. Junior boys have the right to appeal to the headmaster, but the right is rarely, if ever, exercised as there is no use. Dr Arnold's principal innovation was to incorporate the boys of the senior form into the government of the school. Newcomers are required to learn a song and deliver it at their first house dinner; those unable to do so drink a 'brimmer', a jug of foul water from a local well crammed with salt. 'Some of the new fellows are sick for several days.' All wells within walking distance of the school are polluted by cesspits - a persistent bad smell pervades the headmaster's study throughout Tommy's time-hence the habit of the boys drinking beer with their meals. Boys from the School-house wash in a trough in the quadrangle before breakfast and anyone caught not attending to their ablutions has his head held beneath the pump. Williams, a Welsh boy so punished during the winter months, nearly died when the icy flow halted his circulation.

Tommy is in Evans House, a double-storeyed stone building on the side of the close near the island of trees from which Tom Brown watches his last game of cricket at Rugby in the penultimate scene of *Tom Brown's Schooldays*. Tom Brown is now the Captain of the Eleven. With him are his best friend, a gentle refined youth named Arthur, and a verbose young master. Tom Brown is a product of old England, with its hearty squires and sturdy, apple-cheeked yeomen. As a boy, he attended the 'revels', the village games. What Thomas Arnold perceived was that the Age of Industry had gone off like a bomb, destroying village life for miles around each industrial centre, flooding the cities with unwanted people, creating epidemics of crime and disease. Arnold's response was to envisage a new type of leader, young men who could walk down any of the putrid alleys then proliferating in cities across the industrial world, with a firm tread and a steady eye. No-one could make Christians of boys, he said. His task was to make Christian young men. Tom Brown, a self-confessed 'School Tory', has resisted the Doctor's changes, even seeing him as a fanatic. But now he understands. He sees, for instance, that cricket and football are better games than fives, or hares and hounds. They teach discipline and self-reliance. 'The individual doesn't play that he might win, but that his side might.'

A watercolour by Henry Fellows, titled *Football Costumes* 1858/59, shows nine young men standing in front of a rugby goaL One has a moustache; all wear white flannel trousers but have different coloured belts, jerseys and velvet caps. The collarless jersey worn by the boys of Evans House has thin horizontal orange stripes and, on the left breast in black, a two-headed eagle. School-house's jersey has thin red stripes and a large skull and crossbones. Another house has the red cross of the Crusades, another the French *fleur-de-lys*, another the anchor of the Royal Navy; another the thistle of Scotland. These are all potent military symbols of the day. (Old Rugbeians to participate in the Charge of the Light Brigade at Balaclava in 1854 - R.R. Glyn, G.G. Clowes & J.P. Winter. Other Old Rugbeians to distinguish in the Crimea - H.W. Major-General, C.B.; Horatio Shirley, General, K.C.B.; Charles Trollope, General, K.C.B.)

Rugby had an XI in Tommy's day, but not a XV. It took me a while to work that out. As a *code*, Australian football is older than rugby, or, for that matter, soccer or Irish football. In a colony such as Victoria, there was a pressing need for the game to be codified. Otherwise, as J.B. Ellis, 'Fair Play' of the *Argus,* observed, 'any game has two or three gentlemen playing by the rules of different schools and a couple of Irishmen and colonials playing by no rules at all.' George Barnard's watercolour, *The School from the Close* 1852, is a picture of Rugby football in Tommy's time. A group of forty boys is charging at goaL Behind and to the side of them are pile-ups where boys from the opposing house have been knocked to the ground or are being forcibly held down. ('My dear Sir, a battle would look much the same to you, except that the boys would be men, and the balls iron' - *Tom Brown's Schooldays.)* Three boys stand in front of the goal under attack, feet apart, fists raised, braced to meet the final assault. They are the focus of the painting, but their heroism is deliberately understated. In the foreground, closer to the viewer, stand three older students in officer pose, pointing and discussing the game. The boys standing back from the pack and waiting to run with the ball are called the light brigade. The heavy brigade dive into the mauls and do the heaving and pushing. The backdrop to the game is the grand sandstone edifice of the school. The chapel commemorated in verse by Matthew) Arnold is a tall, ghostly grey presence, suggested rather than detailed on the left, while on either side of the game, in direct contrast to its wild unrestrained rhythms, stroll whiskered masters in gowns and mortarboard hats with their wives and small children. 'At Rugby, they lose nothing of the boy that is worth keeping, but build up the man upon it' - Thomas Hughes, author of *Tom Brown's Schooldays.* His book reached Melbourne the year after Tommy and was described by the *Argus* as a manly and healthy work which would serve to confirm the colony's 'natural anti-American tendencies'.

Contemporary criticisms of *Tom Brown's Schooldays* in England: while providing a fine portrait of an individual bully (Flashman), the book did not condemn bullying as an evil *endemic* to the English public school system. 'A boy may have moral courage, and a finely organised brain and nervous system, but he may not possess animal courage and one night's ragging, or bullying, may produce such an injury to his brain and nerves that his usefulness is destroyed for life.' Thomas Hughes wasn't greatly exercised by this criticism, having made it perfectly clear in the book that he didn't have much regard for boys who lacked fight. He simply pointed out that the great public schools of Prussia were no different in this regard. What did agitate him, however, was that Tom Brown's Schooldays had been used as a vehicle for slighting attacks upon his hero, Dr Arnold (the book had been dedicated to his widow). The Edinburgh Review said Arnold had taken the word' serious' and replaced it with 'earnest'. Crueller critics said he turned out bullies and prigs. Rugby boys observed at Oxford and Cambridge, it was said, were a 'solemn array', 'a semi-political, semi-sacerdotal fraternity'. Basically, the criticism of Arnold's system was that it made boys into men before their· time.

A letter from the Rugby school librarian advises that in his four years at Rugby, T.W. Wills advanced only three classes. However, in the same period, his handwriting can be observed to change *extravagantly*. By the time he leaves Rugby, the creaky old wagon of his forehand has been abandoned: he writes backhand! The letters lean to the left like plumes in the wind; each word is a carriage, each sentence a procession, like the 11th Hussars clattering through London in their cherry pantaloons and glittering capes to the wild applause of the populace on their way to the Crimea. In the Rugby XI of 1852 T.W. Wills is last named. In 1853 he is third-named, and in 1854 second-named. In 1855, the year after the Charge of the Light Brigade, he is first-named. Or Captain.

Dr John Bromfield, headmaster,
Melbourne Church of England Grammar School, July 1858

Received Mr Wills, a tall young man with an unduly extravagant handshake, in my study at three o'clock in the afternoon. After we had sat down and taken tea, I asked him if he thought *Tom Brown's Schooldays* provided an accurate account of his old school. 'Pretty accurate, I should say,' he replied with a shrug. His large hands were restless in his lap but I chose to pursue the matter nonetheless, asking him by what means Dr Arnold had effected such a miraculous change in the character of his boys as he is credited with in the book. This question engaged him more thoroughly than the first, and having looked past me and out the window, he said, from what he had been told, Dr Arnold's major change had been to 'take the fellows at their word'. Mr Wills believes a program of organised games is necessary to develop the character of the youth of the colony and, to this end, has volunteered to captain the school in a game of foot-ball to be played in the Richmond Paddock against the Scotch College. In the course of our discussion, he advised me that his last headmaster at Rugby said the study is for Germans, that

Englishmen distinguish themselves in practical arts like statesmanship and war. These words he spoke to me - in my own study! I am uncertain whether he is arrogant or merely devout.

Going to the first match was like going to a real match for me. Caught the train, got off at Richmond, walked along Punt Road. Back then, Punt Road was a track leading down to the place on the river where you could be winched across on a barge. The park was a lightly forested slope. There was game about - emu, bush turkey, kangaroo, lots of bird life. Fresh water in the river below and the three scarred trees. The biggest, on top of the hill between the cricket ground and the road, must have been a mighty red gum. The flesh on either side of the cut bulges where it tried to close the wound, but to no avail. Perhaps youths were brought into the presence of this tree to learn about the duties and responsibilities of age. Who knows? Standing beside it on the day of the first match, you would have looked through a screen of red gums, dead limbs lying shattered at their base, towards a faintly grassed playing field surrounded by a picket fence. The small weatherboard structure with the three-peaked tin roof and five rows of seating on the far side was the pavilion for members of the Melbourne, Cricket Club. The club committee declined to make its playing field available for the furious grind of a football match, having only with difficulty succeeded in levelling the recalcitrant grey earth and sowing it with seed. Instead, the match is to be played among the she-oaks and red gums on the slope above the ground. The day is overcast but at the initiative of the MCC secretary, Mr T.W. Wills, the pavilion has been opened for use by both schools as a change-room. 'The juvenile presbytery and episcopacy came out uncommonly strong.' (the *Melbourne Herald*)

Dr John Bromfield, headmaster, Melbourne Church of England Grammar

Went this day to the Richmond paddock. The game which every newspaper in the colony now instructs me is necessary to the moral health of our young men was a noisy mobile collision lasting several hours. For the whole of that time, young Mr Wills was in the thick of the action, grabbing the ball and passing it out, calling, 'Keep it moving! Keep it moving!' He says needless injuries occur if the ball remains trapped too long in one place. On his chosen subject, Mr Wills is a skilful advocate. When I asked him why injuries should occur at all, he said that eliminating injury meant eliminating the requirement of courage, but that the risk should be equal to all. At Rugby, he saw senior boys insert hardened toes into their boots to dent the shins of their usually younger opponents. These boots they called their 'man-of-wars'.

After the match, Mr Wills was sitting on the steps of the pavilion, his brow wet with perspiration, busily unlacing his playing shoes. I approached him and remarked on the exertion he had undertaken on behalf of the school. 'It is necessary to lead by example,' he replied, and having risen smartly to his feet, left me without another word to further discuss the game with a group of senior boys.

That end of Yarra Park is fringed with oak trees now. Rising above the green foliage, humming with selfabsorption, are the glass towers of the city. And above them? Nothing. Empty blue sky. No-one ever talks about the sky in Melbourne, except to say it's overcast. Originally Melbourne was a water place, a marshy flatland between two rivers. Birds everywhere - big billed pelicans, black swans with curving necks and sharp red noses, gulls, curlews, plovers, ibises, cranes, sandpipers. The Wurundjeri say the place belongs to an eagle. That means eagles once hung motionless in the sky above the marshy plain. Once that was the reality of this place, but now it can only be imagined. The first game was played on the slope between the wall of the stadium and the pink rectangle of the Hilton Hotel. From outside the Hilton it's a short tram ride into the city. I get up, brush the arse of my trousers and rearrange my backpack. Then I head off across the curving slope of the park - the sort of person you wouldn't look twice at, a short, middle-aged man who stops occasionally to imagine what is not there.

Members of the 1859 Victorian cricket team, left to right: Gideon Elliott, Barton Grindrod, George Marshall, Jerry Bryant and Tom Wills.

2

The Great Gun of the Colony

I stand at the centre of the city of Melbourne, on the steps of Flinders Street station. Above my head a dozen clocks tell a dozen different times. Batman's in the pub over the road, head wrapped in bandages to hide his chancres. Once that block belonged to him. Now it belongs to Chloe. She stands, hand on naked hip, in a long gold frame on the pub wall. Soldiers visit her before leaving to fight in foreign' wars, then recreate her image in prison camps and army barracks around the globe. She's Melbourne's nymph. Gulls squawk and eddy, trams clatter past in four directions. The St Kilda tram goes south, across Princes Bridge, squat tribute to the Age of Iron. Each of its lampposts bears the city's coat of arms with the four symbols of its foundation: the Bull, the Sailing Ship, the Whale, and the Golden Fleece. When those emblems had meaning, boiling-down houses lined the banks of the river and the place stank like an abattoir.

The river is flat and slow and the colour of gravy now, but once it leapt rocks and glinted in the sun like brown glass. Six miles from its mouth, above a small rapid, John Batman found fresh water. He had appeared on behalf of Agriculture, there being no more choice land available for pasture in Van Diemen's Land. News of the find fired the interest of a rival consortium. Having survived a turbulent crossing of Bass Strait in his sloop *Enterprize*, Johnny Fawkner landed beneath the rapid and promptly established the district's first business, a public house made of slabs and turf selling high-priced rum in dirty glasses. Melbourne's founding fathers were not a pretty pair. Batman had syphilis and Fawkner had a narrow face and badly scarred back, having received 500 lashes in his youth for attempting to help seven convicts escape Van Diemen's Land in a lugger. Both were sons of convicts, but Batman was native born.

Johnny Fawkner also established the district's first newspaper, the *Port Phillip Patriot*. The muddy settlement, with its dirt roads winding down to the river and problem with half-wild pigs, he grandiosely named Phillipi on the Yarra (he called himself the Tribune of the People, and Batman and his kind the shepherd kings). Others called the settlement Bearbrass. Unfortunately, the authorities in Sydney called it Crown land but they did see the need for enterprise: it takes money to run the biggest prison in the world. Accordingly, Governor Bourke duly made the trip down the eastern coast of the continent in HMS *Rattlesnake* and journeyed up the narrow, treeclogged river. Landing beneath the rapid, Governor Bourke noted an extremely tall white man with a sombre, fearful face lined up with the local blacks to meet him. This was Old Buck. The Governor was told Buckley had survived among the blacks through a fortuitous combination of his inertia and their credulity, a scar on his ankle having persuaded an old gin that he was her long-dead son in spirit form. Governor Bourke and the settlers retired to a tent, business was done and, by nightfall, Bearbrass and Phillipi on the Yarra were no more. In their place stood Lord Melbourne, an ineffectual old fart who liked seeing young women given a good spanking. A pity, I always thought. Bearbrass is one of those bright, bold names you find in the Yukon. Phillipi on the Yarra is a grand folly, the sort you can imagine coming across in the American south. The Yanks are better than us with names, I reckon. They're not frightened to grow their own.

By the time young Tommy Wills returned to Melbourne, I Zingari costume in his bag just waiting to spring to life, brigs, schooners, three-masters and paddle-steamers with iron funnels were standing at Queen Street pier three and four abreast. In his absence, gold had been discovered. At Buninyong, Ballarat, Castlemaine, Bendigo, Ararat... Fortune hunters had flooded in from around the globe. Melbourne had been unable to accommodate the immigrants. A Canvas Town had mushroomed on the south bank of the river. Meanwhile, crops rotted in the fields for lack of labourers, and boats were left without crews. When the government sought to control the rush to the goldfields by imposing a mining licence, the diggers at Ballarat staged an armed rebellion which was quelled in a short but bloody engagement known thereafter as the Battle of the Eureka Stockade. When the authorities sought to prosecute the ringleaders, no jury would convict them and the Legislative Assembly, elected soon after had a vigorous radical faction. Horatio Wills, one of the colony's first nativeborn Legislative Councillors, transferred to the democratically elected Assembly at the first opportunity, in 1856.

Until the disturbance on the goldfields the Legislative Council, in concert with the *Argus* newspaper and the Melbourne Club, had more or less run the colony. One of the Melbourne Club's first homes was Johnny Fawkner's pub, but relations between the parties soured after a group of the younger members put an axe through the door of Johnny's office and smashed his windows to suggest their displeasure with an article which had appeared in the pages of the *Port Phillip Patriot*. In those days, club members tended to be the younger sons of establishment families anxious to make a quick fortune in the colonies and return 'home'. On their irregular visits to the settlement, they drank brandy, smoked cigars and fought the odd duel down by Batman's Hill. One even had an Aboriginal servant dressed in livery who rode behind him on his horse. The rural depression of the 1840s dampened the instinct for speculation in agriculture, thereby weeding out some of the club's wilder and more transient spirits, and, by 1858, Sir Redmond Barry, the president of the club, can boast that the club is 'a pure democracy comprised of the best aristocratic elements of the colony.' He means the pastoralists - or, as they are otherwise known, because of the means by which they acquired their huge holdings, the squatters - plus senior members of the military, judiciary and civil service.

The Melbourne Club claims to be the oldest gentlemen's club in the colony. This is disputed by the Melbourne Cricket Club, but only semi-seriously as the five gentlemen who founded the cricket club in October 1838 were among the 23 who voted for 'a gentlemen's club run along London lines' at a meeting at the Officers' Quarters later in the month. The secretary of the Melbourne Cricket Club in 1858 is T.W. Wills. 'The Melbourne club rushed to secure the services of the young champion.' In a match played at the Melbourne Cricket Ground in January of that year, Victoria, under Wills's captaincy, defeated New South Wales for the first time. T.W. Wills is at the height of his power. 'The colony's Tom Brown' is a star in the firmament of Victoria's ideals and. aspirations, but already there are rumblings of discontent in the gentlemen's quarters. *Wills knows no restraint.*

J .B. Ellis, committeeman, Melbourne Cricket Club
(also 'Fair Play' of the *Argus*), July 1858

Wills urges the committee to trial over-arm bowling. When the point was made that this would put the colony at odds with the long-accepted practice in England, he simply replied, 'It has to come. Why not here?' The view was put (by myself) that were a bowler to simultaneously achieve both greater speed and bounce, particularly on the hazardous surfaces that pass as wickets in this colony, the risk of injury to the batsman would be increased tenfold. To this, our secretary responded: 'Sport which has no risk of injury is women's sport.' Wills has no circumspection, nor is his thinking ever of one piece. He proposes a committee to establish a code of rules for foot-ball, saying the Victorian XI is lacking in the requisite hardiness for battle, then discounts the Rugby game, saying it would result in too many injuries if played on hard grounds by men! He says we shall have 'a game of our own'. In a characteristic flourish which could only succeed in injuring the feelings of several of those around the committee table, he then added that the off-side rule was designed by the English for captains who cannot set a field!

Present: Messrs Tennant, McLeod, Smith & Ellis. T.W.W.'s cousin, H.C.A. Harrison, attended, but did not speak.

Two more views of Tom Wills at this time, the first from a person who followed his lead, Alfred Bonicelli, 'Spectator' of the *Melbourne Illustrated News,* the second from someone who didn't-his sister Emily. The son of an Italian father and an English mother, Bonicelli was born and educated in England and arrived in Melbourne during the Gold Rush. A quick spell in the slush of the diggings persuaded him that journalism was a more congenial way of making a living. Tom Wills's return to Victoria, he wrote, could be described in three words: *veni, vidi, vici ...*

Tom Wills, the Old Rugbeian who revolutionised Australian cricket in the middle years of the departing century, was a true leader. He moved immediately to the centre of things, taking in all around him at a glance, and could simultaneously be engaged in an action while standing outside it, measuring the worth of its individual parts. In the first years after his return from England, his constant companion was his cousin, H.C.A. Harrison, who was later to rise to a position of eminence in colonial society. Had it not been for Wills, however, Harrison would have had no entry to our circle as the rest of us were gentlemen educated at the public schools and universities of England and, from what was said, it seemed that Harrison's education had been chiefly acquired in a tent he had shared with his father on the goldfields. The two cousins were most unalike. Harrison stayed at the edge of events, saying nothing unless asked and then adding little that was original, although it became apparent with the passage of time that when Wills was speaking of something he had seen or done in this land he would often say, 'Isn't that so, Coley?', and the younger man would nod to indicate that Wills was speaking for them both. The two also differed markedly in appearance. Wills always looked as if he had just walked in from a storm, red-cheeked and curls awry, whereas his cousin was a handsome young colt, with sleek black hair and cool blue eyes that rarely met one direct. With the benefit of hindsight, however, I would express the difference between them in this way. Tom Wills was a sportsman, with all the command of craft and strategy which that word implies. Harrison was an athlete, a creature of instinct with a will to win as naked as any I ever saw.

It was Wills who first invited me to watch him run. Harrison was challenging for the quarter-mile championship of Victoria, then held by a Scot from Bendigo named Allen, a miner and a professional. The challenge had been set for two o'clock in the afternoon and, by a quarter to that hour, the course was lined with on-lookers, many standing on fences to better their view. The race was to start at the Richmond paddock and be run along Punt Road towards the Yarra River, finishing in the forecourt of the Sir Henry Barkly Hotel. To better study the form, I indulged my habit of viewing the athletes before the race. Allen, a bare-legged Scotsman with a sharp red face, was circling the starting line with clenched fists. Some yards away, in the long trunks and sleeveless silk jersey of the amateur, was Harrison, loosely flicking his limbs, his eyes deceptively vacant. Allen's camp had sought the meeting because Harrison's growing reputation had threatened his professional claim to be the fastest man in the colony with a consequent drop in his purses. To ensure no slur could be cast on Harrison's amateur status the race was being run for a silver cup, but there was heavy betting on either side. My inclination had been to back the professional man, but Wills guided my five pounds in the contrary direction, saying of his cousin, 'If he had four legs, he'd be the talk of the colony.'

When the race began, the Scotsman immediately loped to the front with strong, rhythmic strokes of his arms, like a man fording a stream. Harrison was one pace to his rear, his action steady and constant. At the halfway mark, the Scotsman tested the Melbourne man, suddenly increasing his speed. Harrison stayed with him, neither falling away nor giving show that he could close the gap. With one hundred yards to go, Allen struck his blow, surging away and relying on brute strength to see him home. The gap snapped open to two paces and instantly the voice of the mob was heard: it was as they had foreseen, the amateur was a pretty performer but he had no heart for the battle. Then, with seventy yards to go, Harrison appeared to acquire not speed, but power. I had positioned myself thirty yards from the finishing line. As the runners flashed past me, I saw the fear in Allen's eyes as Harrison came around him. Looking across at the amateur, I observed how easily an untrained eye could be misled by his style. The arms and legs were as loose and free as ever, but the face was trembling with the demand of a terrible exertion. Harrison was running for his life. He was a yard ahead at the ribbon, his head snapping back in pain. As he slowed to a gasping halt, he had one arm extended to keep wellwishers away. This young champion neither desired nor needed the adulation of the mob.

I turned to share my enthusiasm for such invigorating sport with my neighbour and found, to my pleasure, that it was Wills. In those days, it was no small matter to be seen in public with the Captain of the Victorian XI. His eyes were lit with a deep familial pride. 'I told you he could run,' he said. He went on, 'At Rugby, they would have hacked him down.' I always considered it to be no coincidence, given Wills's influence in those days, that hacking was forbidden from the outset in Victorian football.

Emily Wills to Tom Wills, August 1859

Belle Vue, Geelong

Dear Thomas Wentworth Wills,

I like that! - a scolding about manners from a grumpy young mansuch as yourself. You wish to know why I have not written you a letter. Because I am Outside, on my pony, and am seldom Inside writing letters to you or anyone else. I laughed at what you wrote about being given the wrong room at the Parade Hotel and marching in on old MacAvendish and not being able to shut him up but do take more care on the streets at night. Not every blackguard is going to be tricked into mistaking your pipe for a pistol. Mama is well, as are your brothers and sisters

Love &c &c

From Flinders Street station to the State Library of Victoria is a short walk. I cross at the lights and head north, away from the river, up the long rise that is Swanston Street. On my right is a tall, angular sandstone monolith with stained-glass windows. St Paul's Anglican Cathedral. Halfway down its outer wall, his brass head directed towards Port Melbourne - or Sandridge, as it was known in the days when boatloads of immigrants were dumped on the shores of Port Phillip Bay, stands Matthew Flinders. Today, drinkers gather at the famous navigator's feet. I sat and listened to them once. An old wog broadcast a commentary on the state of the nation, how it used to be called England, but now its real name is the United States. 'There's nothing here,' he was saying, his toothless black hole of a mouth twisted with glee. 'Nothing but pisspots like Wally the Pole.' He continued in this vein until another of the drinkers, a younger man with grease-backed hair and pale quivering fists, exploded, shouting, 'If you don't like it, fuck off back to Jugoslavia or wherever it is you come from.' For a moment the air was charged with the possibility, of violence, but as quickly as it was felt it passed, being replaced by an even more frightening sense of absence. The drinkers have only each other. That is Hell, I think. I hurry past.

Cross Collins Street. In a sun picture taken at this intersection in August 1858 (the word 'photograph' hadn't been invented), Swanston Street is a compact of dirt and stone rutted by carriage wheels and edged with mini-aqueducts - wooden gutters nine feet wide. In winter, the character of the former water place reasserts itself. The body of a baby swept from a carriage outside Flinders Street station in a flash flood is found underneath Prince's Bridge; a horse tethered to a post outside the Post Office drowns when its feet are swept from beneath it by a wave of foul water. Melbourne now has its first church spire, the Methodists having been persuaded by an architect that the Gothic form is not contrary to their rigid beliefs, but an English journalist who visits Melbourne around this time later remembers it chiefly for its dust and flies and the way in which its broad, flat streets routinely meet at right angles. The English journalist also notes that the residents of the young colony are 'given to blow'. Five years earlier, laying the foundation stone for both the Public Library and the University of Melbourne on the one day, Sir Redmond Barry said it was a world record to have two such cultural institutions established within two decades of colonisation. In the sun picture, the Public Library is four blocks to the north, on the brow of the rise. The bluestone building behind and to the rear of the Public Library is the Old Melbourne Gaol. 'We are now making history, and the sun picture supplies the means of passing down a record of what we are, and what we have achieved, in this nineteenth century of our progress.' (the *Argus.*)

Another bluestone building in the foreground of the picture, beside the Police Court, is the Town Hall. Since then, it has acquired a sandstone portico. A red carpet spills out of its polished brass doors, down the steps and across the pavement, like a long tongue stretching out to lick someone's behind. Just past the Town Hall a woman has a flower stall. Thick choruses of carnations - yellow, white, blood-red – crowd her dark green cart. She is pleasantly youthful, without make-up. She has blue eyes and a pony-tail of fair hair. I smile at her, hoping to catch her eye and make some cheerful remark. On the trams I spent my days chatting to people. Baffling. Now I spend my days wandering the streets talking to statues. At night, if I drink too much, I can wake up after a few hours with the roof of my mind like a desert sky, nothing between me and the great emptiness, not a thought or an image or a prayer, just a raging doubt. Nothing. Not for people like me. Have to fight my way out of it. Think of the ones younger than me. They've got more to fear. A greater absence to fill. One of the conductors I worked with was a Greek kid called Billy. Loud little bastard, but his tram always felt alive. He could connect with anyone - old people, migrants, Kooris. Now he's at home watching television all day. I go and see him and he's dull and lethargic. I have taken him books but he doesn't read. I'm not sure if he can.

Burke and Wills are on the next corner, about to disappear into the shimmering haze of central Australia. Burke was a fool. When he was dying of starvation and the blacks brought him food, he threatened them with a pistol. Knew nothing about the bush in Victoria, let alone the interior with its arid red plains and shifting horizons. Miss Julia Matthews, the popular soprano, turned down his proposal of marriage the night before he left. How better to win the woman of one's dreams than to risk everything by going where no white man had ever gone? How did he get the job? He had the right credentials. He was a former cavalry officer, a Protestant Irishman, a member of the Melbourne Club. The club found out soon enough the mistake it had made. He left his account unpaid. They had to sue his estate for the money. I laughed to myself when I read that.

Cross another intersection. To the left, Bourke Street Mall - women with prams, young lovers intertwined like ivy, students in white tuxedos handing out advertising bills, acrobats, street performers. Periodically, the multi-coloured sea of people parts to permit the passage of a clanging tram. Look the other way, up Bourke Street, and am met by the Victorian Parliament. Reminds me of a Roman fort, rectangular and solemn, with a set of stone steps that run almost the length of the building. Only half finished. Melbourne's second boom, in the 1880s, came to a shuddering halt before the building could be completed. In his one address to the Legislative Assembly, H.S. Wills asked that members be allowed to read their speeches. The *Argus* describes his speech as 'bravely spoken', but the motion was lost. The rules of the British Parliament were to apply. No record of him ever having spoken again.

Pass cafes, X-rated bookshops, a shop selling bongs, an amusement park for kids with skateboards. The weathered immensity of the State Library of Victoria looms into sight. The great glass dome dominating its profile is the reading room, added in the early years of the 20th century and modelled on the National Library of Congress. The Greek façade, eleven dimpled columns wreathed at either end in leaves supporting a triangular slab of stone - is pure Victoriana. The original design commissioned by Sir Redmond Barry was plainer, more severe: more Georgian. Sir Redmond stands on a pedestal halfway up the steps in front of the building, his haughty head streaked with verdigris and birdshit. A Protestant Irishman from Cork, he sired four bastards by a mistress whom he acknowledged but never married, instead dedicating himself to the upbringing of the new colony. Sir Redmond, president of the Melbourne Club for a record third term in 1858, personally unpacked and shelved the first 4000 books to arrive from London for the library, which was open to anyone over the age of 14 with clean hands. Later, requesting items for the colony's first public art gallery, he warned the purchasing committee in London against the attitude that anything would suffice 'for a colony'; items of an inferior or mediocre quality would be returned. Sir Redmond desired objects which would illustrate the cultivation of 'the civilized mind'.

The remains of his other great legacy to the State of Victoria lie around the corner in Russell Street, beneath the part of the Old Melbourne Gaol formerly used for dumping the bodies of executed criminals. Sir Redmond told the young man in the dock, the son of an Irish Catholic convict transported to Van Diemen's Land, that he was an outlaw who had put himself outside the affections and regard of civilised society and was therefore as wretched as a beast in the field, and sentenced him to be hung by the neck until dead. The suit of armour the young man wore in his final confrontation with the police is on display in an illuminated glass case in the Old Melbourne Gaol, alongside a death mask made of his head after it had been severed from the body for phrenological purposes and shorn of its facial hair. But the young outlaw lives. I saw him the other day in the street, helmet on, pistols blazing and defiant, emerging from the soft white skin of a young woman's shoulder.

From A Record of the Recent Inter-Colonial Cricket Match, Victoria v New South Wales - the Victorian Cricketers' Guide 1859' (probable author-J.B. Ellis)

We left Sandridge pier in the City of Sydney screw steamer at a quarter past two on Friday afternoon, the 14th of January. Capt. Moodie, too well known for his excellent qualities as a sailor and a gentleman to need any panegyric of mine, took charge of as fine a team of them, sinew and manly bearing as ever went forth to do battle on a cricket or any other field, but before the warp was cast off not a few bumpers of champagne were tossed off by numerous friends to the success of Victoria in the all-important contest. Their valedictory cheers were still ringing across the smooth waters of the bay when the more provident of our adventurers descended to explore the interior of the vessel with a view to nocturnal comfort. A few were lucky enough to become one of the quartet of occupants assigned to each cabin, but by far the major part were condemned to stow themselves in a sort of amphitheatre astern, among the luggage and private property of the stewards, and close to the hideous scrunching and vibration of the never-silent screw and still more horrible, though intermittent, clanking of the rudder chains.

As we had dinner before emerging from the Heads, an excellent muster was obtained and the keen appetite with which all hands attacked the good things provided reminded one strongly of the hearty breakfasts partaken of by condemned criminals on the morning of their execution. For a few hours thereafter, either regardless of their doom, or determined as long as flesh and blood would hold together to put a good face on the matter, glasses were drained, jokes cracked and long songs sung; but as the sun went down and a stiff north-easter got up, choruses relapsed into feeble duets and in turn into even feebler solos, while the jests became highly spasmodic and shockingly bad. By ten o'clock, the collapse had become general, and not a single bold cricketer was to be seen other than in a recumbent and limp posture. Next morning, some attempts were made to perform toilets, but with no Adonising effect, for the woeful white cheeks and parboiled eyes contrasted sadly with particoloured caps and the 'newest things' in shooting jackets and trousers. One or two of 'the team' never showed at all until within sight of Sydney Heads, and then with looks that would have made the fortune of any young tragedian. I need hardly say that the nor-easter never left us, but opposed every inch of our passage, but the stout ship nevertheless made good progress, finally putting us into smooth water about five o'clock on Monday afternoon. For half an hour before this event, the cries for hot water and towels had escalated into a chorus but just as we passed the Gap, where the ill-fated *Dunbar* was lost, all the wretched forms that had for many hours been coiled up in misery emerged with just sufficient pallor in their faces to establish their claim to being living creatures. At the outset of the voyage, the ship's company had included four clerics who had boarded the vessel in ample black skirts and irreproachable white linen. The subsequent forty-eight hours had tested them sorely. They, *too,* had been seen leaning, limp and unshorn, over the ship's side, making copious offerings to Old Neptune. Now, with civilization in sight, they were as assured in God as ever. By this time, we were steaming up Port Jackson, with its well-wooded bays and hundred promontories, its rippling translucent waters, here and there studded with green islands, glittering in the full sheen of a westering sun. For sound, we had the honey which dropped thick and fast from the lips of a voluble American who having contracted love at first sight with the cricketers and being - lucky dog - a good sailor, was incessant in his advice to those around him. Upon landing, we were met by a few of the Sydney cricketers, among whom was Capt. Ward; and while a detachment was escorted to Cunningham's, the rest of us betook ourselves to the Royal Hotel. Here, after due refreshment, ablution and a short walk to spy out the land, we turned in for our first good night's rest since leaving Melbourne.

In the morning, practice was the cry, and a muster being made about eleven, a very crazy omnibus (promptly named the Hit or Miss) drawn by three of the most inadequate quadrupeds ever dignified by the title of horses carne to a halt opposite the not go down. As there was nothing else for it, we took it in turns to carry the huge box containing the cricket material, and after as little delay as possible the field was Royal. After what seemed to be an hour's rumbling (the distance I afterwards ascertained to be about a mile and a half), we came to a dead halt at the top of a sandy hill, overlooking the Military Cricket Ground, which was kindly given us to practice on. The horses would never get up the hill again, we were told, so of course they could be marshalled with our captain, Mr Wills, insisting that each man occupy the position he was to hold in the battle to come. The batsmen went in in alphabetical order, each pair being allowed twenty minutes. Notwithstanding that nobody seemed to have got rid of their sea legs and the turf rose and fell, some very fair hitting and bowling were displayed. The effect upon the small knot of New South Wales supporters was evident as, that night, Victorians desirous of putting a little on the match found that nothing less than odds of two to one would be taken. Play over, an adjournment to the Domain was proposed, and we had an opportunity to see how our antagonists were shaping. Here was congregated half the sweldom of Sydney and most of the crinoline, although the strains of the excellent band of the 12th Battalion floating over the rich foliage of the inner Domain had greater attraction for some than the cricket. Then home to dinner, and as early hours were *de rigueur,* shortly to bed.

The eventful morning broke dull and threatening, and about nine o'clock a heavy thunderstorm passed over Sydney, which was succeeded by a steady rain that lasted until high noon. *'Intonuit laevum,'* said a classical friend on the balcony of the Royal Hotel when a clap of thunder passed overhead. Accept the omen. We did, and as soon as the heavens were 'all serene', the Victorian Eleven proceeded to the ground with the calm conviction of winning for the first time in the territory of the foe. At one, a chance of a wet afternoon had blown over, and the sun shone out amiably. The ground, too, dried up as far as the grass went, but was heavy beneath and by no means adapted to show off Elliott's sparklers to advantage.

Having won the toss, Victoria thought to go in first, but as one or two of our opponents were not yet to the fore, a light skirmish with cold turkey and suchlike trifles (excellently purveyed by host Cunningham) was deemed advisable. It has to be said there was some little stiffness between the opposing forces who eyed each other from time to time in a strange, doggish sort of fashion. In fact, this feeling, however it originated, continued to prevail throughout our stay. To speak a little more plainly, there was a lack of the genial and hearty English welcome we expected to meet from the cricketers of New South Wales (which, by-the-by, I should add, was amply compensated for subsequently by a number of the leading gentlemen of Sydney).

By the time the ground was cleared but few minutes were wanting to three o'clock, and as the blue-and-white clad Victorians dotted the sward, en route for their respective posts, bang went the gun from the bay. This was the signal for a hearty cheer from all parts of the ground, which was lustily responded to by the captain and his crew. But, before proceeding to figures, let me say a few words about the ground. In the middle runs a level parallelogram, about 20 yards wide with as sweet a bit of turf - the couch grass of this country - as a cricketer could wish to tread. Many persons have recommended a trial of this couch grass in Victoria where, long before the season is over, it is difficult to get a decent wicket anywhere. On the upper side of the wicket, fifty yards or so of gentle incline lead to a hill which rises abruptly almost to the road which on this occasion was thronged with vehicles of every description, from well-appointed drags and showy tandems to two horse shays and ginger-beer carts. On the lower side of the ground, towards Woolloomooloo Bay, there is a none too gentle declivity, terminating in swamp.

His Excellency Sir William Denison, who took the liveliest interest in the game, was provided with a marquee near the telegraph, and the two legislative bodies had an even more impressive one facing play on the upper side of the ground. The Sydney cricketers luxuriated in a tent contiguous, but our own establishment was situated at the bottom of the ground with the worst view of the ground and no chairs or seating of any kind. Late on the second day, when the fortunes of the Victorian XI were at their lowest ebb, some of the local spectators of 'the baser sort', not content with seeing things going all their own way, assumed an insolence of demeanour and made use of language which they must have brought with them from Cockatoo Island, or perfected while 'working on the reef' in some other sea-girt penal establishment. These remarks are of course applicable only to the cabbage-tree gentlemen, who individually had nothing whatever to do with the game, but judging from the smirks on the faces of those around us I suspect some of them *were obeying orders!* Not a single attempt was made to preserve order. The conduct of these have objectionable persons, upon whom some restraint might surely have been placed, was so outrageous that a removal of the Victorian tent to the upper portion of the ground was found necessary.

As I said before, it was the purpose of the Victorian XI to go in, but as the Sydney men were so long in 'toeing the scratch', thereby allowing the shades of evening to creep on, and the ground to become dry, it was deemed better to put them in ..

SCOREBOARD

NSW

1st Innings	2nd Innings
Capt. Ward c. Bryant b. Elliott 5	c. Burchett b. Wills 0
Howell b. Wills 3	b. Whitlow 8
Hilliard c. Wills b. Elliott 1	c. Burchett b. Elliott 1
W.E. Still b. Wills 3	lbw Hammersley 8
J.L. Beeston b. Bryant 18	Not Out 7
G. Gilbert b. Bryant 1	b. Wills 4
F. Adams c. Thornton b. Bryant 14	b. Wills 4
O. Lewis b. Wills 13	b. Wills 40
N. Thomson b. Wills 0	b. Wills 0
J. Morris b. Wills 0	Run Out 0
J. Kinlock Not Out 5	c. Thornton b. Wills 0
Leg byes 1, wides 3, n.b.(f.) 1	Leg byes 2, wides 3
Total 63	77

Victoria

lst Innings	2nd Innings
J. M. Bryant c. Hilliard b. Ward 0	c. Gilbert b. Ward 32
B. Grindrod b. Kinloch 5	b. Ward 3
A. Burchett c. Hilliard b. Ward 1	c. & b. Ward 26
G. Elliott b. Kinloch 0	Not Out 9
G. Marshall c. Gilbert b. Ward 1	Run Out 5
E.H. Whitlow b. Ward 3	Not Out 3
W. Hammersley lbw Kinloch 0	b. Kinloch 9
T. Morres c. Thomson b. Ward 13	b. Kinloch 3
T.F. Wray c. Lewis b. Ward 0	Not required to bat
J. Thornton Not Out 0	b. Kinloch 0
T.W. Wills c. Adams b. Kinloch 15	b. Ward 8
Wides 0, byes 0, no balls 0	Leg byes 3, byes 2
Total 38 (for 8 wkts)	103

Victoria Defeats New South Wales by Two Wickets and One Run in Sydney!

Letter to the *Argus* from Rev. R.J. Hornsby, 12 February 1860

The mania for bats and balls in the broiling sun now exceeds all rational excitements. The newspapers have now caught this epidemic, and, while scarcely noticing other far more useful games and feats of skill, devote column after column to minute accounts of the matches played by upwards of a hundred different clubs! Whichever way you turn in Melbourne, a cricket ball is liable to smack you in the eye. An English visitor to the diggings in Bendigo informed me that a flying ball struck his horse after a great number of diggers made a cricket-ground of the highway. When he stopped and remonstrated with them, they were insolent. 'Get along with you,' they said. 'We do as we like here. This is not England.' All this is attributable to the Victorian XI and its victory over 'the crack bats' in the elder colony in Sydney. The Melbourne press has been intoxicated by the result, a reporter from the *Leader* recently designating them the 'laurelled warriors', while Mr Wills, the old Rugbeian who captained the side, is everywhere trumpeted as the Great Gun of the Colony.

Tommy's flying, but his father is trapped back here on earth. Why didn't Horatio Wills speak in the Victorian Parliament? Perhaps because his father was a convict. Name Edward Wills (also known as Willis). Age, 19. Occupation, apprentice printer. 'In that, with two others, he did assault John Martin on the highway and put upon him for his watch, one piece of the Realm called a half-guinea, one piece of silver coin called a sixpence, and 18 pieces of copper called half-pence.' Skylarking, said the defence. Highway robbery, said the judge. Scheduled to dance at the Tyburn fair, a slang expression of the day for the excruciating passage from this world that is death by hanging, his sentence was commuted to transportation for the term of his natural life. Departed England February 1798 aboard the *Hillsborough*.

One in three of the *Hillsborough's* convict cargo failed to survive the journey, the 200 who did landing in the same clothes, now lice-ridden rags, in which they had embarked nine months earlier. Having told the British government he could transport convicts to Botany Bay at a price four pounds per head less than the Royal Navy, the captain, a private contractor, had proved that he was as good as his word. Edward Wills's 17-year-old wife Elizabeth and infant daughter Sarah had also sailed on the *Hillsborough*, as passengers. Upon arrival, Wills was assigned to his wife, a not unknown practice but one subsequently interpreted by his descendants, along with the commuting of the death penalty, as evidence of a friend in high places (i.e. the Duke of Marlborough). Edward Wills quickly and busily became affluent, obtained a pardon and was buried thirteen years after his arrival with the usual blandishments accorded to 'wealthy emancipists in the Sydney press. 'Integrity undoubted, generous in all his actions, universally respected,' etc. Six months after his death, Horatio Spencer Wills was born. It is with the children of Edward Wills that the name Spencer first appears.

Not only was Horatio Wills's father a convict, so was his stepfather, the government printer George Howe (also known as George Happy or Happy George). So, too, was his brother-in-law Dr Redfern, one of three surgeons court-martialled for sympathising with the mutineers in the Nore in 1797. Redfern married Horatio's 14-year-old sister Sarah in 1810. Horatio Wills was a product of Sydney's emancipist class, its convict bourgeoisie, a group not unhappy with their lot if the name of Horatio's cousin, Alfred Australia Clarke, is anything to go by. (Alfred Australia Clarke died at the age of 12, taken by a shark off Sydney Heads - our first naval loss?) In *An Australian Pioneer*, Agatha Wills Booth stated that Horatio Wills's stepfather Robert Howe was the person remembered as the Father of the Press in New South Wales. Not so. The man whose passing was noted in these exalted terms was Robert's father George Howe (a.k.a. George Happy or Happy George) and then only in the family newspaper, the *Sydney Town Gazette*, black-bordered, as in the manner of a royal death. Happy George was proclaimed the Primary Editor of Australia, the Progenitor of Printing in the Colony of New South Wales, etc. Far from being the stepson of Robert Howe, Horatio Wills was in fact his younger stepbrother. The exact nature of these relationships is fundamental to the dispute that follows.

After George Howe's death, Horatio's mother challenged his will, arguing that her second husband was of unsound mind when he died and that the marital property had been divided unfairly in favour of his children at the expense of hers. She lost. Robert Howe duly inherited the editorship of the *Sydney Town Gazette* and promptly used its pages to launch an attack on his stepsister's husband, Dr Redfern, accusing him of using his influence to remove a fellow member from the board of the Bank of New South Wales. A Wesleyan of choleric disposition, Robert Howe had previously copped a bayonet in the belly on his way home from church for something he had written. At the time of the ensuing drama, 16-year-old Horatio Wills was an apprentice printer and his stepbrother was his master.

Redfern v. Howe: On 23 November 1827, Robert Howe alighted from his gig in Charlotte Place outside the office of the *Gazette*. Turning, he saw Dr

Redfern striding towards him with a horsewhip. The Surgeon general then proceeded to give Howe a thrashing. The editor countered with a slash of his sword stick only to have it break on the butt of Redfern's whip. Hands raised to protect his face, Howe backed into the offices of his newspaper with Redfern assailing him. In evidence, Robert Howe testified that '20 stripes' were inflicted upon his person. He denied hurling an iron pot at his attacker, but admitted that his wife had come to his assistance with a broomstick. He agreed that Redfern's head was covered with blood but presumed this was from a fall he had against a brick wall and swore 'there were not 20 cracks' made upon it by his wife with the broom. Howe denied the affair lasted more than two minutes, or that he stood on Redfern's back while his wife beat him, but he did admit under cross-examination that a servant had held Redfern's arms while his wife 'belaboured' him. Dr Redfern was represented by the brilliant champion of Sydney's emancipist class, W.C. Wentworth.

Howe v. Wills: Horatio Wills entered the brawl, breaking the grip of the servant holding the arms of his brother-in-law, Dr Redfern. Wills testified Howe later asked him how dare he interfere and struck him in the face. Wills then flung an ink bottle at Howe, narrowly missing him. Wills also gave evidence that nine or ten months earlier Howe had called him into his office, whereupon he had been grabbed from behind by one of the printers and held while his master gave him a beating. In Howe's defence, a number of his employees testified that Horatio Wills swore loudly and often, had once lost a valuable manuscript, complained frequently about his master's food and, one year earlier, had run away to sea aboard a whaler. Horatio Wills received a suspended sentence of 28 days' gaol on condition that he return to his master and behave as an apprentice ought. Horatio Wills was also represented by the brilliant champion of Sydney's emancipist class, W.C. Wentworth.

Five years later, Horatio Wills reappears as the publisher and editor of his own magazine, a vigorous campaigning journal called the *Currency Lad*. It champions causes, such as free access to public libraries for apprentices, and goes to the defence of six sailors from a whaler being tried for mutiny, then a capital offence. The editor knows only too well that the general allowance to seamen of one pound of meat per day is inadequate for those aboard Pacific whalers. The *Currency Lad* takes as its epigraph the following lines from 'Australasia', the poem with which W.C. Wentworth won second prize in the Chancellor's poetry competition at Cambridge University in 1823:

> *May this-thy last-born INFANT-then arise*
> *To glad thy heart, and greet thy PARENT eyes;*
> *And AUSTRALASIA float, with flag unfurled,*
> *A new BRITANNIA, in another world!*

The *Currency Lad* did, however, permit its young editor one conspicuous indulgence, a reminiscence about his youthful adventures which might be called 'The Romance of Uga Tangi'. Our hero, the young Horatio, leaves Sydney in a tub named the *Saucy Gal* which is skippered by a villainous half-breed (have you ever noticed how half-breeds in 19th-century romantic literature are always villainous?), but is saved from his first misfortune by a second, greater one. Shipwrecked on the island of Uga Tangi, he sees his shipmates mercilessly clubbed to death by savages. Rather than submit to such a fate, he throws himself at the mercy of the beautiful princess watching from one side with an old man with a heavily tattooed face. She is Talinga, he is Chief Mattei. Unable to resist the handsome young sailor's entreaties, the princess pleads for his life with Chief Mattei. Her wish is granted. Romance follows, eventually culminating in Horatio being accepted by Chief Mattei as both son-in-law and heir to the island throne. The escape, by night two eventful years later, gives full scope to the, author's descriptive powers as he is pursued by natives hurling spears. The rescue boat has a phosphorescent wake, Talinga's musical voice floats over the water calling to him to return, etc., but the next morning, leaning against the bow of the *May Queen,* Horatio tells his princess to forgive and forget her errant lover and bury her sorrows. He is answering the call of duty. In fact, he is about to get married.

There is no island in the Pacific called Uga Tangi, nor were there any vessels sailing from Sydney under the names of either the *Saucy Gal* or the *May Queen* during the period in question. The Currency Lad with the sparkling eyes and mischievous grin was what is known colloquially as a bit of a bullshitter, but the story was still written for a reason. As a renunciation by the author of his sinful youth, perhaps. Having departed on his mythical voyage aboard the *Saucy Gal,* he has come home, purified, or the *May Queen.* Who's to say there's not some truth at the core of the story, that there wasn't a Talinga with whom Horatio shared some part of his youthful self? All his life, Horatio Wills couldn't resist trying to charm the natives. At 'Lexington', he performed his special dance for the Djabwurrung, bowing to the Sun and Moon, and told the old woman that he was her son, a 'jump-up black-fellow' like William Buckley, lifting up the leg of his trousers and pointing to the scar on his ankle. Later, in Queensland, his charm would prove fatal.

In Victoria in 1858, however, Horatio Wills is a divided man. He is a Victorian gentleman, an elder of the kirk, the president of the local agricultural society, a member of parliament, *but he cannot speak.* The past he carries within himself, as bright as a gold tooth, is that of a currency lad. His first child was named Thomas Wentworth, as in W.C.

Wentworth. (I have learned to listen to names - they keep time, or try to, like drummers in a march.) Horatio Wills is an Australian nationalist. 'Lexington', his property in western Victoria, was named after the engagement fought by the Minutemen and the British Army over the arms cache of the Massachusetts Militia which helped to ignite the American War of Independence. The 1850s are politically active times. There is agitation and voluble dissent; a mob of several thousand march on Parliament House demanding reform of the laws which effectively prevent men of little wealth from owning land while elevating the squatters to the sort of wealth and influence enjoyed by the European aristocracy. The protesters march beneath the flags of various nations, including the Irish, and their band plays the 'Marseillaise'. They boo the offices of the *Argus*, the landowners' paper, as they pass and cheer the *Age*, which took the miners' side during the Eureka Stockade. Reaching the steps of Parliament House, the mob sings 'Rule Britannia', reserving special enthusiasm for the line, 'Britons never, never never shall be slaves' - yet at the same time former convicts, or 'expirees', are being purged from the Victorian public service in a bid to rid the colony of 'the convict stain'. Watson, the old lag who ran the telegraph station on Flagstaff Hill, 'a friendly, communicative fellow', was so dismissed. The next day he presented his library to the Mechanics Institute then went home to his hovel in Fitzroy and shot himself.

These are issues upon which the Currency Lad would have spoken out, but Horatio Wills is no longer in New South Wales. His brother Thomas has been denied entry to the Melbourne Club, an anonymous black ball being cast against his name. Horatio's manner is described by a fellow member of the Legislative Assembly, a young Radical with a reputation for wit, as coarse and seamanlike. He whispers to Horatio across the floor of the house, 'Sing us a sea shanty, Horatio.' It amuses him to see this decisive, red-cheeked ball of energy reduced to abject speechlessness. In fact, Horatio has read Bentham and other major thinkers of his day, but words fail him, he stutters. In his diary he curses both his native tongue, which seems to express itself fluently only in oaths, and his lack of education, particularly in mathematics and the classics. *But my son! May he prove worthy of my experience! May I be spared for him that he may be useful to his country!* He adds; 'I never knew a father's care.'

Alfred Bonicelli, 'Spectator' of the *Melbourne Illustrated News*

Wills called getting drunk having a bushfire ('Burn off the old growth,' he would say, by way of a toast, 'welcome the new'), but on the night of the Victorian XI's historic first win over New South Wales in Sydney he threatened to blaze out of control. It be-

began with him sitting in the middle of the room, cross-legged and bare-footed, clacking a hairbrush against a hearth broom, and accompanying the racket with a flat nasal chant. His right hand was bandaged, the middle finger of his hand having been broken early in the match, but he hardly seemed to notice. After perhaps 20 minutes of this, or longer, he sprang to his feet and stamped about the room, fingers pointed in front of his face like a mask he was peering through. It was as if he were an animal finding himself among a pack of humans for the first time. Most of those present sought to ignore him; but eventually he brought the room to total silence by dropping to his knees and emitting a strange piercing howl.

Rising to his feet, he declared that the sound had been the cry of the dingo, the Australian wild dog. Catching the eye of one of his fellow players, William Tennant, he said, 'You should be glad I made that sound, Tennant, because one day it won't be heard. Dingoes are vermin, you know they have to be killed.' He said the blacks had two names for the animal, one for those who live with humans, one for those who live apart. He uttered the two words, low harsh sounds with wobbling vowels, then laughed in a strange way and said, 'To tell you the truth I've never known which one I was.' A sense of awkwardness entered the room. When Wills was in such moods his behaviour became ambiguous and no-one knew where his true meaning lay. He must have sensed that the evening's jubilant spirit was at risk of being lost because, with the same startling energy, he declared a game of native football would be played forthwith and, to this end, commandeered a settee cushion and organised two teams, the Romans and the Greeks. Of course, no-one could better Wills at the game, which he insisted on playing bare-foot. He had an extravagant leap which he would employ to balance himself momentarily on the back or shoulders of an opponent and thereby increase his upwards reach. Once he and the cushion hit the floor, the rules of the Rugby game loosely applied with the two sides trying to hack the cushion free and run it to one or other end of the room. In the chaos, the leg of a writing 'desk was broken, which resulted in the hotel owner writing a sharp letter of rebuke to the management of the Victorian team and advising it to seek alternative accommodation on its next visit to Sydney.

The number of blacks in Victoria was greatly reduced by this time, and they were rarely discussed. I once tried to raise the subject of their customs with Wills's cousin, Colden Harrison. He received my question as he received all inquiries, courteously but with a frown, as if it were more properly a matter for the office. So much had been written by experts, he said, he was afraid he could not add to the subject. 'We were so used to having them around that we took them very much for granted, as part of the ordinary scheme of things. We were too young to take a scientific interest in their habits and history.' But he did say that Wills was very clever at picking up their songs and could speak their language as fluently as they did, much to their delight.

Rules of the Melbourne Football Club

May, 1859

Officers of the Club
Committee

T. W. Wills Esq — T. Butterworth Esq
W. Hammersley Esq — Smith Esq
Alex Bruce Esq

Hon Treasurer
J Sewell Esq

Hon Secretary
J B Thompson Esq

"Let go the ball"

Goal for Langer

Sketches of the football match, Geelong v Melbourne.

3

Tommy Throws One
(or The Will of the Father)

The newspaper room is around the corner in La Trobe Street. Such a crowded place, so many voices. Mr McKean Buchanan is fulfilling his engagement at the Criterion Theatre, Sandhurst. 'As usual when this actor appears, the most opposite opinions are being expressed about his performance.' A Mrs Sinclair, accompanied by a Mr Sedley, has quit for England in the *White Star.* 'If our correspondent's information be correct a considerable number of creditors as well as friends are lamenting their sudden departure.' A period nicety. Each age is false and frank in its own way. A botched execution at Melbourne Gaol: 'That he was not dead is clear from the fact that he moved and made a squealing noise when he hit the floor. He then had to be carried up and hanged a second time. Surely a proper rope can be found.' Advice on etiquette, the gentleman rides always at the lady's right hand, dead dogs everywhere, north of Lonsdale Street, washed up on St Kilda beach. Odour offensive, particularly to women. Tommy is usually around here somewhere, high-minded and indignant, in dispute with the committee of the Melbourne Cricket Club. T.W.W.'s term as club secretary is well and truly over. Nothing said publicly, of course, but it is apparent that a state of hostility now exists between the parties. 'Young Shannon from London is happy to accommodate the Maryborough Novice, a match can be made by leaving two guineas with the barman at the Sportsman's Arms, Ballarat.' Love poem tended in Breach-of-Promise case, Monster Fish Caught on the Murray, a quote from Aristotle: Man is by nature a political animal.

The *Argus,* 5 December 1859, by 'Fair Play' (J.B. Ellis)
VICTORIAN ELEVEN v. SIXTEEN OF COUNTY OF BOURKE
    This match was within an ace of not coming off, owing to the absence of the gentleman who undertook the captaincy and marshalling of the Victorian XI. Two of the clock had struck, the XVI had mustered in full strength-a circumstance less to be wondered at, given that a quarter of the team were members of the Melbourne club-all was ready for a start, but Mr Wills, the captain, chose to stay away. A tardy apology was brought over from the Richmond ground that Mr Wills had hurt himself. A glance at another match, to be found below, shows that Mr Wills not only made 19 runs, but also was the direct or indirect means of taking 8 wickets on the Williamstown side, the

match being Richmond versus Williamstown. Most considerable is such lack of courtesy, if not ingenuousness. Notwithstanding the defection of Wills, the Victorian XI contrived to show themselves the better men . . . In conclusion, we may suggest that if these Victorian XI matches are continued the public should have something like a notion who the veritable Eleven are to be, and also that there be no disappointment as to the attendance of either captain or men. The Committee of the Melbourne Club are always willing to give their ground for a good match, but are at the same time very likely to resent anything like an insult, tacit or otherwise.

Mr T.W. Wills to the editor of *Bell's Life of Victoria,* **10 December 1859**
CRICKETING DIFFERENCES
Sir,

As Mr J.B. Ellis, the sporting reporter to the *Argus,* has thought fit to call public attention to me through the medium of the columns of that paper, I trust that you will allow me space in your sporting journal to correct a few errors that he has fallen into. In the first place, he says that I undertook the captaincy of the Victorian Eleven, which is a decided untruth. It would have been the height of presumption on my part to have done so without the voice of the Eleven. I would also ask him how often I acted as captain last season, prior to going to Sydney? If his generally retentive memory fails now, I will for his special edification state how often-once, and yet he never took notice of that; Mr Wray, I believe, acted as captain in most of the matches. On Saturday last I merely chose an eleven as one of the match committee. He further states (as much as to say) I was not hurt, and that I only sent over an excuse from the Richmond ground so as to be able to play there. This was not the case:

I was seriously hurt, and have not improved myself by playing there. He further states that the Melbourne Club know how to resent an insult, etc. I would ask him what the Melbourne Club have to do with the Inter-colonial match? Is this illustrious fixture actually a club fixture?

The matches of the Richmond Cricket Club were all arranged long before the Eleven were thought of being chosen, and if I was ever so well I would not desert it in the hour of need for any match. Besides which, I calculated that the eleven that were chosen were perfectly competent to beat the sixteen that were brought against them, and the match, as far as the bowling was concerned, would not have been very much practice, as it is not very likely that we will have either Mr

Hammill or Mr Cameron against us on the 2nd, 3rd and 4th February next. Did the *Argus* reporter call a general meeting of the Melbourne Cricket Club on Saturday to learn their opinion of me, or does he give his and their ideas from his private note book? (The one that incommodes his fielding, I mean.) I also beg to state that as I feel that I cannot conscientiously act on a committee of which he is a member, I have sent in my resignation to the committee of the Intercolonial Match, fully determined to have nothing whatever to do with the arrangements of the match; but should the match committee think me worthy of a place in the Victorian Eleven, I shall be happy to contribute all I can towards winning the match. I also resign my position on the match committee, from an idea that in case this very impartial reporter should not be chosen I might be blamed for partiality, as he evidently deems himself as a great gun' (report in *Argus* of Monday). Woe to the Victorian Eleven if her team are all such great guns. And in conclusion I beg to state that there have been more rows between clubs and cricketers since Mr Ellis has had anything to do with reporting matches than is good for that friendly feeling which should exist between cricketers; he is, in fact, quickly gaining for himself the hearty dislike of the cricketing community. Trusting, sir, that you will allow this to go forth to the public, to show them that at least I do not quietly stand by to hear of myself being snubbed by a vindictive reporter, who cannot take the venom from his pen even when writing an account of a friendly game, I remain, yours,

T.W. Wills

Trouble in the club. Such a succulent phrase. So suggestive of licentiousness and mild villainy. The Melbourne club, too. The establishment does not care to have its differences aired in public, but then it has never had anyone like Thomas Wentworth Wills to deal with before. 'In this colony alone, he donned the colours of the Melbourne, Richmond, South Yarra, Williamstown, Emerald Hill, Corio and Geelong, clubs *(to* name but a few). He even played with the blacks ... ' And, eight times out of ten-I have scanned the records-the team he played for won. T.W.W. is observed in the street around this time, eyes both seeing and unseeing, his fine clothes looking slightly shabby, 'as if they represent an idea that no longer interests him'. His enemies on the committee of the Melbourne Cricket Club say he is vainglorious and incompetent. This is William Tennant many years later: 'When Wills left the office [of the Melbourne Cricket Club], everything was in a muddle, club papers, books, cricket balls, cricket guides, Zingari flannels, cigars, spiked boots all stuffed together in one large tin trunk. He was a most untidy mortal and quite unfit for such work.' In reply, Tommy declares that the committee members of the MCC possess 'the tiny sight of insects trapped beneath a rock'. He is alone in his battle with cricket's governing bodies - alone, that is, but for the mob. They call him Tommy and speak as if he were one of them. Privately, his critics say this is because he drinks even more than they do, but that is not what is being said in public houses like the White Hart at the top end of Bourke Street. There they say Tom Wills is without fear. Batted for five hours in a temperature of 107 degrees Fahrenheit at the Melbourne ground, refusing to retire, then collapsed upon his return to the pavilion. Revived with smelling salts, he flung his arms about 'like a man who has been rescued from drowning'.

The *Argus*, 3 April 1860, by 'Fair Play' (J.B. Ellis)
MELBOURNE v. COLLINGWOOD

A run of ill luck seems to be attending the Melbourne club. Beaten easily by Richmond a short time back, they were on Saturday compelled to cry *peccavimus* to the Collingwood club, although taking the field with a very strong team. Wills, the migratory, was found in the Collingwood ranks and, as usual, he returned proud figures. A great deal of his bowling was, however, unfair in two respects - it was too high in the first place, besides bearing the closest possible affinity to a throw. The umpire for his side took no notice whatsoever of these continued improprieties, notwithstanding the repeated cries of 'No ball' from the pavilion, which was crowded with members of the Melbourne club and their friends. This is by no means the first time this season that Wills, who ought to set a good instead of a bad example, has transgressed the tenth law. In the Intercolonial Match he put in a shy every now and then, and last week at Emerald Hill was frequently much above his shoulder, His motto seems to be: 'Get wickets honestly if you can but-get wickets'. It is not to be expected that young bowlers, when they find 'the captain' sin with impunity, will be troubled with any rigid scruples, and bad habits will be acquired that will take a whole season to get rid of. (Wills 52 balls, 3 maidens, 6 wickets, 15 runs.)

Mr T.W. Wills, in reply, to the editor of *Bell's Life of Victoria*, 7 April 1860 -
MORE CRICKETING DIFFERENCES
Sir.

I daresay it is in your memory that some time back the Richmond club were rather roughly handled in the columns of the *Argus* for .allowing the 'Plebs' to express their delight when sundry good and bad specimens of cricket were exhibited on the Richmond ground, as if the public were under the management of the club, but nothing has been said through the columns of that paper touching the uncricketlike and ungentlemanly conduct of the Melbourne club and their friends who patronised the match played on their ground last Saturday between the Collingwood boys and the great MCC. It was a curious coincidence that on the morning of the Intercolonial Match when I appeared to be rather late upon the ground, some of the very men who were so uproarious against my bowling on Saturday came up to me and said, 'We are so glad that you have come-we thought you had left us in the lurch,' and another remarkable feature occurred on the second day of the grand match when the Sydney men fell fast before my bowling-there was no cry then raised against my bowling; oh no, sir, it would not have suited them then; not it; but when their pet club gets into difficulties they have no lack of friends to shout and bellow 'no ball', thereby endeavouring to bias the umpire, and who would on that account be perfectly justified in allowing anyone to bowl however high, if he thought fit, having by this sort of behaviour had his honour called into question. And this is the Melbourne club, that wishes to be thought *facile princeps* in all matters relating to cricket. The reporter in the *Argus* stated that I bowled sometimes high, and at other times shied, yet to neither of these improprieties did the umpire of the MCC pay the least regard. I should like to know, Sir, what was the greater impropriety, my bowling high or otherwise, considering that I had an umpire to judge me, or the members and their friends bellowing like madmen, considering also that they had no umpire to judge of them, save and except the cricketing public. Trusting, Sir, that when the MCC again plays with boys they will teach them the manners of gentlemen, I remain, yours, etc.,

T.W. Wills

Where's Horatio? Three floors up in Rare Books engaged in religious meditation. Others in the colony, whom he calls capitalists, exalt in their riches and have no regard for the First Cause. 'I am happy to say that my mind hourly becomes more familiarised with religious impressions.' He is seeking to subdue his filthy native tongue. Swearing is incompatible with the duties of a Christian gentleman and he is working to excise it from his language. 'I feel it is necessary for 'man to suffer much worldly misery to induce him to look beyond the things of this world.' His diary entries are marked by crescendos of religious exaltation during which it seems he can scarcely control himself. 'O God Most Holy O God Most Strong O God O

God O God.' No mention now of the romantic island of Uga Tangi, and still less of the dark Talinga and her wifely charms. The only seas Horatio now admits to having been lost upon are the seas of youthful passion and it is his wife Elizabeth, not the crew of the *May Queen,* who saved him. 'Without her mild Christian virtues, I should have been a barque lost in the tempest. She has been the star of my destiny. From a wild youth, she has centred my affections on our domestic hearth, & long may they continue to blossom there.' But, still, he fears his past. 'The heart of man is deceitful above all things & desperately wicked!' To the end of his life, a young woman will visit Horatio in his dreams to warn him of imminent danger. In his diary he calls her his 'thing'. Of course, Agatha Wills Booth tells us she was a white lady.

Out riding, he shoots a sparrow hawk for no reason other than idle speculation about the accuracy of his shot, then sees the poor creature's tortured writhing on the ground and knows that he has offended God. Arriving home, he finds that Little Joe, his pet kangaroo, has been missing since Monday. Tall Boy, his dog, the best in the district, expired in his arms the previous week. 'God's will be done & these are not large things, but it does make one fearful. *'Coming events cast their shadow before them;'* He has reduced his tobacco intake to one pipe per day, taken after the evening meal, but is still compelled to make use of laxatives. 'Inside I am tied!' Horatio Wills is blocked. He curses his lack of education. 'Vain regret! When a youth, anxious for information-like the mariner without his compass-I wandered here and there, & the only knowledge at which I have arrived is that I am unable to influence any activity other than my own!' He continues the reading list he has been compiling for Tom since he was a boy. Bentham is of interest, Byron too fanciful to give real satisfaction, John the truest Gospel. 'Read last night the life of Ali Pasha-another lesson for ambitious men. Read it Tom!' Ambition is folly, he tells his son. 'Libraries are crammed with volumes telling of the follies and ultimate disappointment of ambitious men.' The chief aim in life of a Christian gentleman is the cultivation of domestic affections. 'A Christian marriage is as close to the Divine as any man can get in this world, Tom!' He reapplies himself to his domestic responsibilities and tells himself he is pleased to do so. One of his children suffers a near-fatal attack of croup. Horatio investigates the illness with his customary vigour, making out two pages of notes based on his readings. 'I trust that all my children who marry will take a copy of these instructions & leave them in the toilet drawer.'

He was at his desk investigating new methods of irrigation when he received a letter from his eldest sister Sarah, formerly Mrs Redfern, now remarried (Redfern died in 1833) and living in London, informing him that she had just returned from Rugby, having seen Tom. Her nephew had stayed with her upon his arrival in England. She thought him backward and advised Horatio Rugby might not accept him. Now, two years later, having returned from a visit to the famous school, she counselled Horatio to leave his son there because of the effect it was having upon his character. He was becoming a gentleman, tall and well spoken. But she did not shield her brother from her concerns. 'I fear something necessary to the intercourse of the world is missing from Tom. He has no aspirations beyond the playing of cricket...'

HORATIO WILLS TO TOM WILLS, April 1854

Your letter came to hand yesterday, and, as with all letters from you, gave considerable satisfaction. I note with interest the details of the sermon you sent me and the scores. You still however continue to write with a scrawl that would make a writing master eat his nails, and there are occasional errors in spelling and in grammatical construction of your sentences at which I am much surprised. If you cannot write correctly now I am afraid you never will: After all my trouble, are you going to turn out a dunce?! At your age, with all the means at your disposal, you should be able to write in English correctly and well, to write and talk French, and have a pretty fair knowledge of Latin. You must strive to accomplish this as soon as possible, for you must shortly commence your studies for a profession. The law is the most honourable-the merchant also has a fair time of it. If you have brains take the law. Come out here 5 or 6 years hence a barrister. Remember that everything you do is for yourself, and if you do not succeed in life and obtain the reputation of a clever gentlemanly fellow, no one will be to blame but yourself...

He tried. Remember? T.W. Wills-first in Repetition. Said the lines so often he ground them into his skull, returning to Victoria-as we are told by virtually every source-with the stamp of Rugby and Cambridge fresh upon him. Unfortunately, there is no evidence he actually entered the famous university's portals, the records merely indicate that he played for Cambridge against Oxford in an intervarsity cricket match. Two months later, he was in Dublin playing for the First All-Ireland XI (other varsity gentlemen to participate in that game: R. Hankey, Ox.; R. McCormick, Cam.). In the same twelve-month period, he also played for the Gentlemen of Kent and was invited to tour with an All-England XI. Duly arrived home, champagne glass in hand, in the costume of the I Zingari club. I Zingari are the gypsy lords of English cricket, a team of aristocrats who play by night as well as by day. Soon in debt. The worst sort of gambler, I suspect-the sort who can't imagine losing. William Tennant, "Pine Leg' of the *Australasian,* put it this way: 'With his excessive confidence, Wills never despaired of fortune favouring his cause even when fortune was most against him.'

An apprenticeship with a Collingwood solicitor, organised by Horatio, falls through. In a letter, Tommy tells his brother Cedric that a legal apprenticeship involves *'too* many years in another man's service'. This decision drives his perplexed father beyond the limits of his patience. Horatio Wills had judged Rugby to be the great public school of the day, the one best attuned to the new age, which anyone with half a brain could see was dawning throughout the civilised world. Now he finds that the young man who has returned to him, so assured and so magnificent in some ways, is wholly deficient in others. *I had better schooled him myself!* Horatio Wills believes in lawful authority. In the past, he has taken a stick to a drunken shepherd to show him who was master. T.W.W. is summoned home to Geelong. He labours with the smithy in the forge, fashioning wheels for carts, and spends long hours bent double in the humid heat of the shearing shed, shaving fleeces from plump merinos. What is conspicuously absent from this episode is any evidence that Tom, now aged 25 and an acknowledged leader in his field, *ever questioned his father's authority!* Was the father's attitude pre-conditioned by the fact that the son may have been prone to mild attacks of epilepsy? William Tennant said Wills possessed 'an infirmity'. T.W.W. to Emma Wills, October 1857: 'I have felt beastly bad this last week. When anyone speaks to me I cannot for the life of me work out what they are saying-everything seems so curious.

Tommy sends the results from the Geelong Athletic Sports, along with stamps, to Cedric in Germany. His letters to the sporting press are spears forged in the flames of his indignation. His letters to his siblings are streams of consciousness-usually the stream that will get him to the bottom of the page quickest and with the least effort. Another brother, Egbert, won the juvenile 440 yards, first prize ten shillings. Tommy entered the half-mile but did not start as he was given only 3 yards start of a man named Stevens from Melbourne who had been training for three months. 'Pa writes & says you have struck one of your masters. If such a thing were done at a Public School in England you would be expelled & the disgrace would cling to you throughout life not a very enviable thing to have said about one certainly [his words frequently pile into one another] besides which it makes Pa angry & causes Ma great annoyance & if you do so again Pa will send for you back and besides it sets a bad example for your younger brother, so I trust that in future you will be on your guard.' Colden won the high jump with a leap of five feet, first prize 30 shillings, Tommy won the drop kick with 173 ft. 'Not bad for a muff, eh? do you see any old Australians?'

Horatio meanwhile departs for Europe, satisfied that he has finally settled Tom into meaningful employment. No sooner has the father gone than the equally irrepressible son re-emerges as the captain of the Geelong Football Club. I quote Aristotle: The temperament of the athlete is not necessarily conducive to the duties of a citizen. During the Gold Rush, Geelong had been closer than Melbourne to the booming gold town of Ballarat and to the squatters of the western districts. Billing itself as the Pivot of the Colony, Geelong fancied its chances of wresting the mantle of capital from Melbourne. Its football team call themselves the Pivotonians, and chooses to devise its own rules rather than submit to those of the Melbourne club, with the result that the Geelong team is soon renowned for wanting to run 'with the ball in hand'. Six months after T.W. Wills joins their ranks, the Geelong club are the Champions of the Colony and their captain is described as 'the pillar in the team which cannot be toppled'. There is said to be a special joy in seeing 'the marriage of technique and timing that is Tom Wills punting the heavy ball'. As in cricket, he plays with eyes that see everything and a face that reveals nothing, 'the better to mask his guile'. As yet, however, football is no more than a diversion, a couple of hours of crash and bash among the gum trees on winter afternoons. The main game, the one which carries the possibility of Imperial recognition and honours, is cricket.

The *Argus*, 3 December 1860, by 'Fair Play' (J.B. Ellis)
MELBOURNE V. THE UNITED XI

To be 'run out' is not pleasant, but a 'professional' man should not set a bad example by losing his temper and saying, 'They won't catch me playing again.' Umpires give curious decisions sometimes, but when declared 'out', a player should not throw his bat on the field and assault people afterwards. If we are to have cricket in this colony-if we wish to enjoy a visit from the great 'Eleven' of England-by all means let our cricketers imitate their confreres in the old country and check those ebullitions of temper which have too often marred great matches here. Tom Wills was bowled fairly-we do not hesitate to use the word. If a man stands with his bat behind him-if, when bowled out, he gives three different versions as to why he did not take guard-then there can be no doubt that the matter should be considered final, and that a scene discreditable to Wills and injurious to the club should not again occur ...

T.W. Wills to the editor of the *Argus*, 4 December 1860
Sir,

I am accustomed to being misrepresented, but in the above match I have been harder dealt with than ever before. Your reporter says, or at any rate pretty plainly intimates, that I threw my bat down while at the wicket, and afterwards assaulted people. I simply deny the allegation. On the contrary, upon being told by the umpire that I was out, although I had my bat behind my back as a significant intimation to the bowler of non-preparation, I went away quietly, and as a cricketer should, towards the pavilion, bat in hand. What may have occurred afterwards matters not. Suffice it to say that enough provocation was given me to act even more as a 'muscular Christian' than I did. I am not now asking you to reverse your reporter's decision as to my being in or out, as that is a matter I would rather leave to a cricketing authority, but simply to exonerate me from a charge of discourteous conduct on the ground . . .

Your obedient servant,

T.W. Wills

[With reference to the above letter, our reporter states that Mr Wills 'did' throw his bat on the ground whilst walking from the wicket; that he did afterwards 'assault' people; and that, whether through 'provocation' or other causes, which Mr Wills apparently forgets, he behaved himself in a manner wholly unworthy of what he really is - a good cricketer. As to his' muscular Christianity', if he refers to more than one gentleman present, no doubt they can tell him that he gave practical illustration of it in a manner by no means pleasant or acceptable to them.-Ed.]

Where is Horatio now? Almost at the bottom of the Irish Sea. At the end of a tour of Europe that included a visit to his sons Cedric and Horace in Bonn (‚Remember my boys work hard for yourselves as your Papa has worked for you'), Horatio crossed to Ireland, visited the lakes of Killarney and, suitably for the author of 'The Romance of Uga Tangi', kissed the Blarney stone. Returning to England from Ireland aboard a paddle-steamer, he is caught in a terrible storm. One sea causes the globe in Horatio's cabin lamp to jump from its base and smash upon the floor, another extinguishes the binnacle lamp. It is a night when a dozen vessels are lost. 'Most passengers lie in their cabins, too ill even for fear, listening to the wind screech and howl and trying to think of something other than the steamer's pitiless pitch and roll. Not the old Pacific whaler. Alone among the passengers, he climbs to the upper deck 'to better see the wildness of the night'. Realising that for the first time in 25 years of sea-going he is about to be sick, he moves to the lee side of the steamer but, as he does so, the wind whips up his cloak, wrapping it round his head. Unable to release himself, he staggers about blindly, hitting lifeboats and cabin walls. When he eventually extricates himself from his cloak, his face is smeared with dribble and vomit, and he is laughing. The Victorian Gentleman stands unmasked, his wet round face lit with a fierce, transforming joy. Lightning splits the ink-black sky to the west. He laughs even more loudly, a long crackling noise that imitates the elements. 'I never had so grand a night in years.' Once all things surrendered to his energy and charm, but for the past decade, Horatio Wills has sat in the House of Sly Talk, as he calls it, robbed of his power. Selling 'Lexington', he now sees, may have been a mistake. Victoria's gold reserves cannot last. Having toured Europe and seen the sophistication of its industry, it is now apparent to him that the basis of enduring prosperity in the colonies is property. While he is so absorbed, the wind slackens and the sea is pacified. Other passengers now emerge from their cabins pale and shaky, to find a drenched, rotund man standing on the upper deck beaming, his youthful self renewed. 'Thanks be to God! I see His hand in all Things!'

It is after Horatio Wills returns to Geelong that he is paid a visit by William Wills, the young Englishman who is to accompany Robert O'Hara Burke on the Victorian expedition shortly to leave Melbourne on camels in a bid to cross the Australian continent, for the first time, from south to north. Victoria is under threat from a new colony to its west. Called South Australia, it has had no association with convicts whatsoever, and loudly advertises the fact. It has also sponsored a succession of successful expeditions into the interior under the leadership of Mr Charles Sturt. William Wills, the son of a doctor, has an amateur interest in the natural sciences. A deeply introverted young man, he comes to pay his respects to Horatio, whom he calls a great Victorian pioneer, and to seek advice on the sort of difficulties the expedition might reasonably expect to encounter. The two are not related, but Horatio is greatly impressed by the young Englishman's earnestness and diligent attention to detail. In the wake of William Wills's departure, H.S. Wills decides to act. 'We want difficulties to animate and entertain us! With nothing to occupy the mind, human beings feed upon themselves.' At the age of 50, he will strike out anew for the frontier which now lies more than 1000 miles to the north in the recently proclaimed colony of Queensland. Like the expedition of Messrs Burke and Wills, his party will be the best equipped and largest of its type to have left the colony. And, this time, Abraham will take Isaac with him.

From the Last Will and Testament of Horatio Spencer Howe Wills, dated 3 June 1861

... in the event of my said son Thomas Wentworth Wills misconduct-ing himself and his conduct and management of my said station on the Nogoa River (otherwise known as Cullin-la-ringo) being of such a nature as to make it necessary for my said Trustees, or the survivors of them, the executors, administrators and assignees, to remove my said son from the management of such station and in his place appoint any other person or persons to superintend or manage the same AND in the event of my said son being removed I hereby declare that he, my said son Thomas Wentworth Wills, shall not participate in the final distribution of my estates but in lieu of his part or share shall receive for the term of his natural life the yearly sum of One hundred pounds and no more ...

I like to leave the library after dark, particularly when it's been raining. The melaleucas that border the library steps are fragrant with spice and the wet black floor of the city is splashed with neon colours. This is the moment of the day I most enjoy, watching the trams rumble past, north and south, making their heavy metallic music, while on the pavement people hurry horne singly and in pairs. Standing there, half hidden by the dark, I feel part of this quaint, distinctive city with its store of ghosts and memories. In fact, where I am standing is a movie set. In Stanley Kramer's film *On the Beach*, protesters gather on the steps of the State Library of Victoria to declare their opposition to the madness of nuclear war. A nuclear cloud is enveloping the globe, poisoning each country and city in turn. Melbourne is last to go. The film ends with the final protest, a banner hanging limp as a sock, not a human being in sight, everybody either dead or too ill to attend; then someone, maybe Kramer, croaks into the microphone, 'It's not too late.' I want to believe that. Sir Redmond Barry is in *On the Beach*, as are Joan of Arc and Saint George. But the penguins aren't. A year or so ago, there was a flock of emperor penguins in front of the library with black nib-noses and orange bibs on their white fronts the colour of egg yolk. Of all the statues, they were my favourite, but vandals came and decapitated them in the night.

4
Cullin-la-ringo

I was 13 when I first came to Melbourne on my own, entering through the western suburbs, crossing the Maribyrnong River-originally called the Salt-water to distinguish it from the Fresh-water-and arriving at Spencer Street station. Flinders Street station, in the centre of town, is the colour of old cheese, golden-brown, with arches like giant eyebrows and a silly green copper helmet of the sort the Mongols wore. Spencer Street is a brick shed alongside rows of flat platforms with men in green uniforms pushing trolleys. I was met by my mother's brother, a small, ginger-haired man with a foul mouth and an alcohol problem, whom I took to immediately. With him, I went to my first game of league footy. Never seen anything like it. My uncle, beer can in hand, standing on a platform made from the cans he had already consumed, shouting, *'Who's gunna fuck ya missus tonight, Patterson?'* Patterson, number 14, was Essendon's lumberingly heavy and devoutly Methodist full back. My uncle broadcast for the entire match, mostly in the form of a dialogue with two Fitzroy players, Butch Gale and Kevin Murray. Gale, the Fitzroy captain, he alternately urged, implored, abused, congratulated and, finally, commiserated with. Kevin Murray received completely different treatment. Toothless and tattooed, with a ranginess that seemed to equip him with both strength and agility, Murray was Fitzroy's champion. He wasn't the biggest man on the field, but he played as if he were. My uncle spoke about Kevin Murray in the way that other men speak about a favourite car ... when they see their reflection in its much-polished bonnet.

Afterwards we went to a Brunswick pub, another first, and he stationed me in a corner with a lemon squash. There was such warmth in the noise that surrounded me, the grey hum of voices, the sparks of laughter, the chink of glasses. I asked my uncle questions about Fitzroy and he showed me a photo he carried in his wallet of the player he said was the greatest in the history of the game-Haydn Bunton. In the photograph, a slight, dark-haired young man was leaping through the air, ball beneath his arm, right foot pointed forward, left tucked in behind. Earth nowhere in sight. I said he looked like a god and my uncle nodded and said, 'Yeah, you could say that.' For me, at the age of thirteen, the greatest place on earth was Melbourne on a Saturday afternoon, standing in a crowd watching this recklessly athletic theatre with its occasional moments of startling grace, then afterwards going to pubs and listening to the stories. So few stories where I carne from. There was only me and Nan. She was like an old tree. Each evening I landed in her branches, each morning I flew off again. Mum blew in every twelve or eighteen months, always about to start something new, and Dad was never mentioned. The only item of family history I ever received was that Nan's grandfather, an Irishman from Cork, was a trooper on the Victorian goldfields.

I now know that he came via Van Diemen's Land, the recipient of an assisted passage from the British government for stealing meat at the height of the potato famine. If Nan knew about his lagging, she never breathed a word. But just occasionally, when she'd had a glass of stout, an unspoken fury would flash in her eye and she'd say quietly, 'Don't let the bastards get you down'. I won't, Nan, and thanks for the advice.

In. my 20s I went to Europe, and saw England, Scotland and Ireland with the vague expectation that the last of these would feel like home. It didn't, not in the way that the Brunswick pub did when I was a boy. It was almost as if I couldn't speak their language. Different rhythm, different speed; my language bespoke a great flatness. I went to the Soviet Union after that and had the benefit of seeing a totalitarian state in operation, then travelled through Scandinavia in a train, increasingly conscious of a great loneliness at the core of my being. Like a sickness. Ended up in Africa with dysentery and half my hair gone. Went to a camel market in Khartoum feeling lost and exhausted and met a Collingwood supporter complaining about Wayne Harmes being outside the boundary line when he knocked the ball back into play during the closing minutes of the previous year's grand final. Never thought I'd be pleased to meet a Collingwood supporter, but I was. Came home and felt doubly baffled. How could I call this place home? Its great spaces assailed me with their emptiness. The land was said to have sacred places but I knew neither their whereabouts nor how to recognise one if I were to stumble upon it. Thought then that perhaps the idea of home is an illusion, a yearning we carry through our days like hunger and thirst to keep us in a necessary state of motion. Thought perhaps the best response to life was a certain stoic calm, then went to the footy, saw the Krakouer brothers and yelled my head off.

The Krakouers were two Nyungahs from the southern tip of Western Australia. Not big men-the size of lamb pizzles, an English journalist wrote when they played in an exhibition match in London-but with an understanding that was like nothing anyone in Melbourne could recall having seen. Not only did each know where the other was, he knew where the other was going to be four or five frames later in the action. Jack Dyer, one of the older generation of commentators, got it right. He said, 'He's the best player I've seen, the Krakouers.' Each week, the Krakouers unravelled the game and reinvented it while people leaned across the fence and spewed hatred on them. Don't know why, but I took it personally. Began getting into arguments. At the same time, I started seeing there was another system of thought at work in this land. Phil was the younger brother, Jimmy the older, but if anyone hit Phil, Jimmy evened up. Then or later didn't matter, Jimmy left no debt unsettled. He had his own law.

The Warlpiri tribal lands east of Alice Springs could be in northern Africa; the country is red and bare. I went there in 1987 for the so-called Black Olympics-the Australian football carnival attended by traditional Aboriginal communities from throughout northern and central Australia. A photographer I knew agreed to take me along. My first sight of Yuendumu, where the sports are held, was of humpies and rubbish and mangy dogs with worn hides and bad eyes. A white nurse we met said six communities hadn't come. Wouldn't say why and became visibly agitated when pressed by the photographer. Neither of us thought about the black man standing beside her. Eventually, she hissed, 'It's men's business. Don't you understand?' The Pitjantjatjara were initiating young men in Dreaming paths and where they crossed roads it was the roads that closed. The Law was being practised in full seriousness, the dreaded Red Ochre Man was about. Three days later, just as the grand final was about to begin, a child ran into the crowd saying she had seen an old man with a red headband. Within 15 minutes, players, umpires and supporters had disappeared. The lot. A ball was left spinning in the middle of the dirt oval. Sophisticated folk from the city say they don't understand these things, but, believe me, they do. The fear, white-hot and startling, is sufficiently strong to reconnect modern man with the strangely intimate world of his own ancient prohibitions. We are older than we know.

Perhaps as many as ten different language groups were present at the sports. For two days, men and women sat unmoving around the lip of the red-dirt oval while the game flowed past them like a river. Some of the players had boots, some didn't. The tackling was hard but measured. Why? I asked. Ground too hard, I was told. Fair enough. Then, late on the second day, two players from neighbouring communities abruptly exchanged blows. In an instant, two groups - perhaps two or three hundred people -were on the field, boomerangs and spears in hand. Injury had been done. The matter would have to be settled that night, blackfellah way, which meant armed combat. The umpire told me that. His mother was a Warlpiri woman, his father a passing Irishman. Taken by the authorities because he was a child of mixed race, he'd been sent to an orphanage in Adelaide. After twenty years of doing okay in the white world, he'd returned to the desert, observed the deep silence of his people's relationship with the land and felt his loss. Briefly, this blackfellah with Irish charm and I shared an affinity.

Central Queensland I saw in a drought year. The few rivers were putrid pools of green water and the grey mud on their banks was shiny hard. In the paddocks the black soil had curled and split and the only fodder was clumps of brittle yellow grass. As a region, it didn't have the grandeur of central Australia. The shapes pushing through the earth had a red, raw, unfinished feel to them. Here and there were hints of the tropical-bottle-shaped boab trees, a shiny green shrub on the sides of hills with a broad, sharp leaf but otherwise the scrub was dry and featureless. Even in a car, there was something dispiriting about coming over a rise and seeing yet another hot, yellow, empty space that had to be pushed against and opened like an invisible door. On the back roads, dust hung like a curtain of grey air behind each passing vehicle. In a pub in Rockhampton I was told that in the old days the same journey, from Rockhampton to Springsure, took three days. Brisbane to Springsure took three weeks. My drinking companion, a man about ten years my elder, was both hospitable and cheerfully racist. He knew the blacks. He said they were all right so long as you kept them in their place. He was also for secession from the south. 'From Canberra?' I asked, but he laughed and said, 'That can come later.' He meant Brisbane. I knew then I had crossed a border. Brisbane, like Darwin, had always been on the far north of my imaginings.

John Moore, shepherd, 1861

> Leaving Ipswich, we made stages of 10 miles, 3$^{1/2}$ miles, 6 miles. One of the bullocks died of heat exhaustion in the yoke. After that, the Governor decided we would camp by ten o'clock in the morning and travel by the moon. Our party was the biggest that had ever ventured this far north, 32 bullocks, two drays, four tons of goods, ten thousand sheep and the wool press. Ned Quinn said the wool press reminded him of the guillotine of the French. Had great work in ascending the Main Range, not reaching our camp (called Toowoomba) until 10 at night. Climbing the Scarface Range, we nearly lost a dray. Eighteen bullocks on and three drovers when she broke from her moorings, a chain snapping just as it reached the summit. It dragged the four after bullocks backwards, the eyes in their big brutish faces bulging with fear. The wool press caught against a tree, otherwise over the bank would have gone dray, bullocks and all. The Governor kept saying it was a grand thing we were doing. 'What an adventure!' was his cry. There was nothing the Governor could not do. He chased the bullocks, rounded up the

horses, boiled the billy for his son's morning cup of tea. He even delivered Mrs Baker's baby daughter when we were one month into the journey. Then two pups died of distemper and Henry Reid drowned fording Gatton Creek. The Governor said Henry was as good a man as he had ever had. Two rams fought, and one wandered off into the scrub groggy and dazed where Ned Kenny lost the run of him. The Governor was most displeased. He missed nothing, did Old Mr Wills, and there was no task to which he did not lend his hand, unlike his son, Master Thomas, who stood to one side, looking red-faced and saying little.

Unbeknownst to the Governor, some of the young gentlemen in the party had gins obtained for them at stations along the way. There was talk as to whether this was wise. Rainworth we reached in August. The manager of that station was a young English gentleman with the soft pale skin of one who had not long been in the colonies. His name was Gregson and he told the Governor he should be wearing side-arms. The Governor replied, 'I don't think that will be necessary.' 'It's a policy with which all my neighbours concur,' said Gregson, whereupon the Governor replied, 'I have been dealing with blacks since before you were born, young man. I will allow they require firm treatment but they also respond to kindness.' Gregson had shot some blacks for stealing sheep only just before. 'I have had my last sheep stolen,' he said. 'The native police assisted me to deal with the matter.' After he had gone, the Governor told us we had nothing to fear, that the blacks in these parts were even more backward than those in Port Phillip. He said that when he was surveying the property the previous year he had been approached by a black who thought he and his horse were one creature! He also said a group of them stole a rifle and placed it in hot charcoals to make it spit fire as they had seen it do when held by a white man. When it went off, killing one of their number, they thought it was the devil. We all laughed at his story.

Gregson had said we should make it understood to any blacks we encountered that they were not permitted in our camp, but the Old Man greeted them with tobacco and blankets and boiled sweets for the children. By day, the Governor allowed the blacks, to walk around our camp, insisting only that the males shield their nakedness from our womenfolk. To this end, he gave the bucks lengths of calico, demonstrating how the cloth should be worn about the waist in the manner of a skirt, completing the display with a small dance in which he pretended to speak to the sun. The next morning, much to the amusement of the young gentlemen in our party, the natives solemnly reappeared, each of the men with his length of calico knotted around his shoulders and trailing behind him like the Lord Mayor of London's cloak. The Governor spoke sharply then, and shouted at their leader. The blacks continued to visit, lifting lids and looking into tins and boxes. The Governor said they were just being curious like children, but the night after we arrived on Cullin-la-ringo I heard Master Thomas arguing with him in their tent. Young Mr Wills said Gregson was right. He said we should be carrying weapons at all times. I heard him say, 'Papa, the natives are not friendly.' The Governor said something about his experience of the blacks in Port Phillip and young Mr Wills replied, 'This is not Port Phillip, Papa! We are as far from Port Phillip as the Crimea is from London,' but the Governor laughed and said he would hear no more of Master Thomas's boyish imaginings. The next morning, I observed young Mr Wills teaching Mrs Baker how to point a revolver.

Tombstone, Rockhampton cemetery
WILLIAM NEWBOLD

Died March 2nd 1868, aged 21 years, From the effects of wounds received in pioneer warfare.

Pity him, stranger, thus cut off in early youth whilst in the discharge of his duty and in obedience to that earliest of God's commandments, 'Go forth and subdue the earth'.

From 'Mr Edward Curr's National Inquiry, for Ethnological Purposes, into Aboriginal Vocabularies and Dialects', conducted on Cullin-la-ringo station, Queensland, circa 1879

one-*wungarra*   two-*booZ-a-roo*   three-*booZa-roo wungurra*
blackfellow-*mar-die*   2 blacks-*mardie booZaroo*
white man-*meek-a-Zoo* God-*unknown*

Agatha Wills Booth

Separation Creek, the boundary between Rainworth and my grandfather's new property, was crossed on the 49th anniversary of my grandfather's birthday. Rainworth station was at that time the outpost of civilization. Pushing forward another three miles, the pioneers reached a small but pretty creek where they formed their camp on a high piece of rocky ground above the water. As soon as the camp was settled, the party began building brush yards in which to fold the sheep, in order to avoid the necessity of watching them at night. A few days later, my Grandfather rode out to look for timber for building purposes and met a black gin carrying a piccaninny astride her shoulders, with his tiny fingers firmly clutching the gin's hair. This is the usual manner in which the natives carry their babies. The woman was much alarmed at seeing a white man, possibly the first she had seen, but because my Grandfather wished to be on friendly terms with the natives he got off his horse' and bound a silk handkerchief round the piccaninny's head. This pleased the lubra and shortly afterwards they parted as friends, although neither understood a word the other had said. For a few days matters progressed quietly and without untoward event; then some blacks made an appearance at the camp. They 'were treated kindly and given presents. The next day they returned, bringing others with them, and in a few days there were a great number about. As the blacks gathered, they formed their camp in a patch of scrub at the foot of the nearest mountain about a mile from the tents. The whites were now becoming so accustomed to the blacks that any feelings of fear they may have had gradually wore off, especially as the blackfellows also came into the whites' camp unarmed. On a number of occasions when the blacks were loitering about the camp my Grandfather amused himself by shooting a few of the 'numerous hawks which are always to be found hovering around any settlement in Queensland. His object was to show the blacks the use of the gun and its deadly effect. My Grandfather had an excellent supply of firearms, and he frequently suggested to the men that they should be prepared always-for emergencies; but the men were in no way afraid or suspicious.

Transportation difficulties had made it necessary to leave one of the drays behind on the road many miles distant. My Grandfather now decided to send his son, Tom, with a couple of men and a team of bullocks for it. The next morning when one of the men was mustering the bullocks on foot he was quietly surrounded by about fifty aborigines, and to his great alarm they closed in upon him, took off his hat and felt his body all over; but because they used no violence, and allowed him to go immediately they had completed their search of him, he soon recovered from his fright. Upon returning to the camp, he told my Grandfather and his companions what had happened to him. The consensus of opinion was that the blackfellows were influenced by curiosity only. However, before my Uncle Tom left the camp, he went to all the men who were to remain behind and asked them to carry firearms at all times. He feared trouble but, without exception, the men expressed their confidence in the trustworthiness of the natives and said they could obtain their arms from the tents the moment they were needed. As Uncle Tom was about to leave, my Grandfather shook hands with him, a thing they very seldom did on the road. He was worried because the 'white lady', a premonition which had come to him since early in his life, had visited him the night before in his sleep. 'Goodbye, old fellow,' he said. 'Be back as soon as possible for I am always uneasy for you while you are away.'

Horatio Wills's last letter instructs his wife to place a public notice in the *Geelong Advertiser* announcing the safe arrival of his party at Cullin-la-ringo on the Nogoa River 200 miles west of Rockhampton after a journey of eight months. 'Notwithstanding rains, roads, rivers 'and scrubs, not one of the party suffered sickness.' Not one, Horatio? Remember Henry Ford? As good a man as you'd ever had. Drowned fording Gatton Creek. 'The country for a long distance around is open and magnificent.' The notice has the brisk, optimistic tone of someone for whom the real work is about to begin. It is further evidence that Horatio Wills failed to perceive the fundamental difference between the western districts of Victoria in 1850 and central Queensland a decade later. He wasn't dealing with a defeated people. Is that what the woman in his dream tried to tell him? Did she sense the natives' silent rage? Could she see what he was so intent on overlooking? 'Labour is scarce and at high rates. Shepherds 30 shillings a week, bullock drivers from thirty shillings to two pounds.'

'Westward Ho', an article from the *Queenslander* of 15 January 1931. A photograph of five low flat hills at the end of a plain outside the town of Springsure. From left, Mount Spencer, Mount Horatio, Mount Howe and Mount Wills. On the right, between Mount Wills and the fifth hill, Murdering Gap. I came from the north, leaving a dirt road to wrestle with a wire gate and then bump across a drought-stricken paddock, its black soil split and cracked like over-baked clay. Reaching a dried-up creek rimmed with desiccated trees and prickly shrubs, I dropped back to first gear, dipped into the river bed and accelerated up the far bank, sand billowing from the wheels of the utility. I stopped beside a small coolabah tree. Tommy came from the opposite direction, creaking dray packed and loaded, bullocks swaying to their laborious rhythms, a boy of 13 for company beside him and a driver with a whip walking ahead. Perhaps they talked cricket. George Elliott, brother of Gid Elliott who opened the bowling with Tommy in Sydney two years earlier, was in the party. No doubt a bat and ball was somewhere among the luggage. But that sort of talk could have only lasted so long and then, once again, they were inching their way across the dry, hard plain. Tommy knew something his father didn't. The blacks were not friendly. He knew because he had had black friends. One of those on Cullin-la-ringo had stolen his father's pith helmet from off his head. Horatio played along, performing his silly dance, bowing to the Sun. and Moon, thinking it could not fail to win them to him. But with these people, there was a distance that could not be bridged. Even words spoken in their own tongue evaporated into the air. A bullock team proceeds at walking pace. Any shadow behind any tree could have been a black man with a spear, or .a number of them. In a few years, there would be small wooden forts dotted throughout this district. Any white man who was attacked would gallop madly to the nearest of them, secure himself and his horse inside, then fight for his life, shielded from the spears. Eventually, the five flat-topped hills appeared, their sides flushed with the strange pinkness of northern Australia. Passing through the gap, what awaited Tommy was the sight of men on horseback, only one or two known to him. Then the campsite, charred and smoking. Boxes open-knives, forks, items of clothing, papers, all strewn about. Two large mounds of freshly dug earth. All eyes both upon him and trying not to look.

William Thompson, Nogoa River grazier, 19 October 1861

The following bodies were found:

1.   Mr Wills at his tent door. A deep tomahawk wound in his right cheek, the neck being nearly cut through below the same spot his privates swollen and evidently severely beaten.

2.   Margaret Manion, a girl apparently about ten, her head beaten with a waddy and a tomahawk beside her.

3.   Also a female infant of Mrs Manion's

4.   Mrs Manion dressed-wounded in the head with waddies and   tomahawk beside her.

5.   Her daughter aged about 5 or 6 years-died of sundry wounds and lying beside her undressed.

6.   James Scott-cook-found speared in the belly with spear still sticking in the wound also terribly beated about the head-not undressed.

7.   Elizabeth Baker lying at the door of the tent partly undressed killed by blows on the head, her hair covered with blood.

8.   A boy, son of Baker the overseer (Elizabeth's brother) killed by blows on the head-also an infant female.

9.   Also daughter of Baker apparently about seven months old killed by a blow on the head with a waddy on other side of same tent.

10.   Mrs Baker -partly undressed-killed in the same manner.

11.   Near a bough fence about 50 yards from the tents was found the body of Patrick Manion stripped to the waist, his head deeply wounded with a tomahawk and beaten in with a waddy.

12.   About 20 yards off and within the fence was found the body of a bullock driver who had on a flannel shirt, his trousers taken off, killed by deep tomahawk wounds and blows from waddy.

13.   Further around the same fence was found the body of George Ling, bullock driver. Dressed. Killed with tomahawk wounds and waddy blows to the head. A pocket book was found on the ground near the fence belonging to David Baker.

14.   Baker, the overseer, and 15, his son David and 16, a man known as Little Ned (could be Edward McCormack) were found about a mile below the head station where they had been camped out with the ewes and lambs - all murdered by tomahawk, waddy and axeblows.

17. Henry Pickering, a very old man, was found about a mile out on the plain from the head station where he died from wounds apparently inflicted by the same weapons.

Mr Wills we buried by himself. The rest we buried in a common grave about 50 yards away. The ground around was much trodden and covered with scraps of clothing and calico. In some places, the grass was burnt by sparks blown from the galley fire, the coals in which were still burning. Stolen: clothes, private boxes, books, papers, crockery, tools, blankets, axes, tomahawks, knives, etc. All the dead presented a harrowing appearance. Their bodies were in positions which showed they had been killed on the instant without any struggle. Mr Wills was at the mouth of his tent, revolver in hand. It seemed that he had responded to the sound of the disturbance but only got one shot off before being overpowered. The presence of gins and children would seem to indicate that the attack was not premeditated, but was suggested by the unwary and practically defenceless state of the unhappy sufferers. Two still missing - George Elliott who was with the overseer Baker, and a labourer known as Michael who was shepherding at the head station. In the afternoon, while so engaged, young Mr Wills, who had been several days down the track collecting provisions with a dray, returned and was taken to the place where his father was buried. He dropped to his knees but no sound escaped his lips.

Three weeks. Three weeks for the news to be relayed: from Cullin-la-ringo to Rockhampton, from Rockhampton to Brisbane, Brisbane to Sydney, Sydney to the Union Bank in Geelong. *Horatio Wills, Mamas & and 8 others murdered by blacks at Rockhampton. Send word to friends immediately. Steamer for Rockhampton next week. NB. Word 'Mamas' may be 'Thomas'.* Four days later: *Horace Wills, Mrs Baker daughter and two (2) children, Mrs Manjon and three (3) children & Scott murdered on 20th instant by blacks. Tom Wills safe.* In all, forty telegraphs, forty pieces of paper bearing the Imperial coat of arms and conflicting information over a period of several weeks. Unbeknownst to Horatio, his wife was pregnant when he left. Their youngest child, a one-month-old daughter, is seriously ill with diphtheria. *Rockhampton Morning Bulletin:* 'Another Frightful Massacre By The Blacks, Native Police Proceeding to the Area'. *Sydney Morning Herald:* 'The slaughter of 70 blacks in the reprisal raid cannot be justified except upon reasons which point to the annihilation of the race. How was it determined who was innocent and who was guilty?' Elizabeth Wills to Cedric and Horace Wills in Germany: 'How could any of the blacks be innocent? They all knew. Did one not cry out, "Me no kill white fellows", as he was shot?' Emma Wills to her brothers in Germany: 'Tom says he will shoot all the natives that ever show their face and he hopes his brothers will do the same as the blood of their father cries out for vengeance from the breast of Cullin-laringo.' Tom Wills to Colden Harrison one week after the massacre: *I am in such a state of bewilderment I scarce know what to write.*

Alfred Bonicelli, 'Spectator' of the *Melbourne Illustrated News*

By the end of his long career, Wills rarely spoke except to issue instructions. In the field, he was characteristically to be seen between balls with his head down biting a fingernail to the quick or chewing upon a curl of whisker. He also became bald, which lent a comic aspect to his appearance, rather like a reticent schoolmaster whose passion is the First XI.

Agatha Wills Booth, *An Australian Pioneer*

After consultation, it was decided that the drays should be loaded and Uncle Tom should take the sheep back to a spot six miles from Rainworth Station as he was not in a fit state to participate in the pursuit of the murderers. A party of eleven men led by Mr Gregson then started in pursuit of the murderers. The tracks were followed easily, except occasionally where they crossed patches of rocky ground. When the party reached the Nogoa River, they came upon a heap of articles which had been left behind with the apparent intention of returning for them at a later date, as they were covered carefully with sheets of bark stripped for the purpose. The trail was hot, and about two hours before sundown the blacks' camp was discovered in a patch of dense scrub near a mountain now called Snake Range, about twenty miles from the scene of the tragedy.

Early on Wednesday morning the search party quietly surrounded the blacks and awaited daylight. One of the party had been left behind a short distance in charge of the horses. It was agreed that the leader of the Whites should have first shot, and the members of the party anxiously awaited daylight. As day broke, the blacks started to get up and start their fires. One blackfellow stood up with a paper spread out in his hands, as he had. seen white men do, for they are born mimics, and pretended to read to the others. The incident caused some merriment among those who were awake; but little did he know vengeance was so near. At the very moment he was acting the he-man, the leader of the search party was taking deadly aim, and the still of the morning was suddenly broken by the loud report of the rifle. The blackfellow, paper still in hand, fell dead. All was now confusion, but it lasted only a few minutes. When the shooting was ended several blacks lay dead, where a few moments before they had all been sleeping peaceably. This was the first lesson taught to the blacks for their treachery, and many more of their number were to fall before the gun ere the lesson was learned that the murder of white men did not pay.

The White Party now returned to Rainworth Station, where they found a detachment of native police under the command of Lieutenant Cave, who started in pursuit of the tribesmen on Thursday 24th October. The punishment meted out to the murderers was very severe, and of the many who took part in the massacre very few lived to tell of it. Still the lesson had not been learned. For a long time, nearly every year single murders were committed in the District, but in almost all cases the victims were isolated shepherds. These murders were followed up, always, relentlessly, the native police reporting the' dispersal of a camp of blacks'.

From 'Select Committee Inquiry of the Queensland Parliament into the Native Police (1861)', evidence of Lieutenant Frederick 'Filibuster' Walker

Q. You have no written or printed instructions?

A. No printed ones.

Q. In what way then do you act?

A. I act according to the letters I receive from squatters.

Q. Do you not think it right that you should be cognizant of the facts before you take your measures?

A. If a man has been murdered or sheep or cattle have been stolen, I generally go to the station, go to the proprietor of the station - and ride about it, and pick up tracks.

Q. Do you think it right to pursue these blacks say a month or so after the depredations?

A. Well, yes, if you can be perfectly certain of the facts a month afterwards, I have always acted immediately - whenever I have been called upon, I have gone up to the station immediately.

Q. Do you not think that these depredators should be captured?

A. You don't know who they are, it is the tribe you follow - you can't see the depredators.

Q. When you go to a camp do you call upon them, in the Queen's name, in any way, to surrender?

A. No, because directly they see you they run. You have to gallop to get on to them. If you were to call upon them to surrender, you would never keep them in sight.

Q. Do you not think there is any other way of dealing with them, except by shooting them?

A. No, I don't think they can understand anything else except shooting them; at least, that is the case so far as my experience goes.

T.W. Wills petitions the Queensland Government, requesting a permanent police presence in the district-'otherwise shepherds will not stay for fear of attacks by the blacks.' Simultaneously, he tells his mother to invest. Stockyards and storerooms are needed & shepherds to assist with the lambing. 'The lamb's make the station-nothing else. The shearing after next I predict we will shear 18,000 sheep, the year after that, 40,000.' One of Gregson's men has scurvy very bad, but Tommy's men have huts and can at least live like Christians. 'You will see by my calculations, which are most minute, that the only way to safeguard the property, given its vast size, is to invest.' Mr Donald, from Peak Downs, says Tommy's' yards are the best in Queensland and Mr Donald is going to erect yards after his plan. 'The only sure path is to invest.' Tommy has sworn on his father's grave to make Cullin-la-ringo the best station in the colony. Then, a sudden cry of pain-'Why have I been BURDENED with Mr Roope!'

T.W.Wills is not entrusted with command of Cullin-la-ringo. Instead, 61-year-old William Roope, the husband of Elizabeth Wills's sister, has been assigned by Horatio Wills's trustees to manage the station. Roope arrives, pink and fastidious, with a barrel of porter which he permits his nephew to share with him on the basis of one glass per day. 'Roope is an old fool. He takes everything upon himself-the men and myself then have to redo all he has done, or rather not done. Baker, the foreman, is a great help, he sets the men a good example by working well, but Mr Roope doesn't like him because Baker says Mr Thomas would not do this or that, as the case might be. Roope tried bullying him which is the last way to keep good men in a place like this.' Six months later, defeated by the heat, Roope leaves, declaring his intention to administer the station from Rockhampton.

When does he leave? The most critical time - lambing. 'So much for his experience gained 8 & 20 years ago at the North Pole doing I don't know what.'

Alone again, T.W.W. renews his appeals to let him begin developing the station. 'A good shed is needed, one that will last 4 or 5 years, or else lambs will be lost-Even if they have to borrow the money, it can be repaid.' In the midst of writing, he is called away to deal with a trifling matter in the store. 'If Ced were here he could look after it.' His younger brother has been summoned home from Germany and is expected at Christmas. 'Has Ced arrived Yet? He will arrive when all the work is done, lucky cove, but I will find a job for him tho', like making a wash pen down on the Nogoa River.' He pleads with his mother to invest. 'There is no risk in what I propose as the expenses are far under what Mr Roope calculated, as can be seen from my most minute calculations.' He begs and bullies, whinges and whines. 'If the trustees insist on adopting half measures they better sell at once although it would be a sin-Father would not have sold for any sum even if he had to borrow for a good start.' Horatio's fatal misadventure has left the family's fortunes dangerously exposed; his proposals are ignored. Tommy's stylish backhand becomes wilder, eventually flipping over into the forehand of his semiliterate youth like a yacht in a high wind. There is a good chance the writer is roaring drunk.

'What is the point of owning SHEEP if one does not have the necessary labour to deliver the LAMBS!!!! Borrow by all means, don't sell this Great Fortune, or else I shall say my Father's children are not worthy to bear HIS NAME!' From his sister-despite the suffering he has incurred on the family's behalf-he has heard NOT a word! 'My Sister is the very essence of I don't know what and I'll never write her again as long as she remains Miss Emily or Mrs Anybody else.' Since Tommy's departure from Melbourne, Colden Harrison has fallen in love with Emily and is paying her court. 'Can't get time to write she says why it's such a pack of nonsense from beginning to end has she not got every evening of the week-she can find it convenient to write to others as I hear, no time complained of there OH NO MISS EMILY!!!!' Tommy is shouting with all his might so that people 1000 miles away will hear him; but no-one is listening.

In the end, he is talking to himself. Sandy blight in his right eye, God willing his sight will be restored. No woman to share his load or mend his clothes. Can't sleep for fear of attack. Trustees won't trust him with money but thank God he does his duty to his poor Father & when he and Ced finally get their share they will thank no man except their poor dear Father who gave them such a gift. 'So go to work Tom & Remember your duty & your poor dear Father's words and work like a man.' Wild dingoes came in the night and savaged his dog Jimmy on the chain. Tore out his throat. Ice nearly an inch thick in the morning but the day soon as hot as ever. Walking to the sheep yards looked down snake coiled around his leg, glistening and evil. 'My father that God trusted, I only act now as if he himself were present! have named the hills near the old camp Mount Horatio, Mount Spencer, Mount Howe, Mount Wills.'

From 'Mr Edward Curr's National Inquiry, for Ethnological Purposes, into Aboriginal Vocabularies and Dialects', conducted on Cullin-la-ringo station, Queensland, circa 1879

Have they any superstitions; if so, what?
They think the spirits of departed relatives hover around their camp when they sleep.
track of foot - *dee-na*
dark - *gnor-coon*
moon - *car-car-da*
ghost - *woo-kin*

Two last letters to do with Cullin-la-ringo. One from Tommy to Ced as Tommy gleefully departs the colony for a cricket match against a touring English XI in New Zealand. Tommy presumes his younger brother is coming to act as his second-in-command. He's not. He is coming to take over. At the age of 22, Cedric Wills will overland 10000 wethers from central Queensland to Swan Hill in northern Victoria. Initially with the help of Horace Wills, the third brother, but later alone, he will nearly save the huge property for the family before being beaten by the drought of the 1890s when the bank forecloses on the mortgage. Cedric lacked the Currency Lad's largeness of personality-he was feisty and dour-but he was every bit as capable as Horatio. Unlike poor old Tom with his grand, unworldly visions. Unless there was a bat or ball involved, there was no point asking Tom. That's what people said. In Geelong, it was rumoured that he had to be removed from

Cullin-la-ringo. Money missing from stations accounts, unauthorised expenditures, etc. No more sheep on the property after two years than those his father arrived with.

> 21st December 1863 Rockhampton
> My Dear Ced,
> I arrived here (a Brute of a hole) on Tuesday last the Straightsman had left on Monday & today the James Patterson is in & leaves on Thursday morning for Sydney & I'm off like a shot-our 2nd order of goods have not arrived about 4 Ton 15 cwt at the stores for us: all our wool came in Friday last, wool all in good order altho some of the bales had large holes in caused by rubbing against each other. but otherwise all in good order Sheep at the highest here will only bring 15 shillings a head & Bennett will give that for either 1500 or 2900. There is a letter at the post for you none for me-I was sitting the other day under Mr Rutherford's Verandah & who should come along but old Roope & Mr Rutherford said, 'I have just been shown part of a spear that was thrown at Mr Riddle'. Roope said, 'Who shows it to you?' and the answer was, 'Mr Wills here' -Mr Roope turned around & stared hard at me and said Bless my soul you are not Tom Wills, and I said, I used to be at any rate-after some time he got up in rather an excited state and said, 'Mr Tom Wills, you have not been doing your duty to the Memory your father-you have let the blacks come up to your station' -I simply said I was not aware of the fact, & he replied that he was-I said again, very well, you know better than I do-So he walked off
> Sell a mob of sheep, 1500 if you can @ 15 shillings a head-it is a good price
> I remain
> Your aff Brother Thomas W. Wills
> PS I shall have a hard race to make the first match in New Zealand

From the Union Bank, Geelong (trustees of the estate of Horatio Wills), to Cedric Wills, Cullin-la-ringo, 20 February 1864

Dear Sir,
Your letter of the 16th January I have duly received. I wrote to you the same day as Mrs Wills had shewn me another letter relative to your Brother Thomas and finance matters-

By my letter you will see that the Trustees are under a precaution to prevent any trifling with Station funds and for this cause mostly they have an Agent at the Station. I am glad to find H.H. & Co have not honoured any cheques drawn by your brother without Mr Johnson's Signature.

You are right as to the Trustees possessing powers under the will to remove Your Brother from the Station. The will is at the lawyers and I cannot get it now to send you the Extract you wish-Your brother has been to New Zealand with the Cricketers and I believe is daily expected back. Neither the Trustees nor myself have seen him since he left the Station. You may rest assured that the interests of the Estate generally will be watched over and no irregularities in finance matters will in any way be sanctioned.

I am

Yours very truly, W.E Ducker

Most people end Tom Wills's story there. Remembered for his contribution to colonial cricket, etcetera. But there is more. At least one whole Act. As evidence, I would tender a photograph marked 'Melbourne Cricket Ground Boxing Day 1866' taken of the Australian Native XI prior to the start of its match with the Rest of the World XI. Eight thousand people in attendance.

The only bigger crowd in the history of the' colony was four years earlier when H.H. Stephenson's first All-England XI played a Victorian XVIII. The English team's carriage was blocked by cheering well-wishers when it arrived in Melbourne and, the following day, 15 000 people of all classes-or one in eight of the population-gathered at the Melbourne Cricket Ground. When no more spectators could be crammed into the ground, settlers on horses, gentlemen in top hats with women in crinoline dresses, families in traps, and some of the city's many stray dogs gathered on the slopes above the playing field to vie for a glimpse of the action. Urchins climbed into the tops of the red gums. A long, canvas-covered grandstand at the Punt Road end of the ground bore the name of the tour promoters, Bourke Street restaurateurs Spiers and Pond, who later bought a restaurant in the West End of London on their profits. No-one anticipated the wild success of the First All-England Tour, the cricketers only having been invited after novelist Charles Dickens declined an offer of 10000 pounds to do a reading tour of the Antipodes and provide the sort of novelty entertainment which flourished in Melbourne during the Gold Rush at venues like the Hippodrome and La Salle de Valentino.

The match between the Australian Native XI and the gentlemen of the Melbourne Cricket Club, playing as the Rest of the World XI, is seen by various interested parties as the first step in launching a reciprocal tour of

England by a team of Aboriginal cricketers. A ladies' marquee, decorated with nautical pennants and erected alongside the members' pavilion, is alive with chatter and the clinking of glasses. A military band plays, lively airs from a nearby rotunda. The crowd is inquisitive, most never having seen a black before. Part of the interest in the team is that they are seen as specimens of a dying race. In the photograph, six of the Aboriginal cricketers are seated, with two standing at either end and two behind. They are wearing coats, waistcoats and white cotton trousers; in their hands are the flat-topped hats they sport on the field of play. One has a bow tie, another a cravat. Their names, as listed on the photograph are, back row, Tarpot and Mullagh; front row, King Cole, Jellico, Peter, Red Cap, Harry Rose, Bullocky, Cuzens and Dick-a-Dick. All are bearded except Jellico, who is young and bare-faced, and Harry Rose, who has mutton chops. Listed as absent from the photograph are Watty and Paddy. The Aboriginal cricketers look handsome but sombre. Two weeks before, they were in their traditional lands in far western Victoria. Now they are about to embark on a four-month tour that will take them as far north as Sydney and Newcastle, and already one of their number, Sugar, has died away from the place of his ancestors, leaving his spirit lost and alone. The captain of the Australian Native XI is in the middle of the back row. In contrast to his team-mates, his appearance is scruffy and he wears a cloth cap to shield his growing baldness. His face is like a dried-up river bed. Some say he is doing it for the money; he is known to have debts. Others say he is forgiving to a fault. He says nothing. Tom Wills no longer expects to be understood.

The Aboriginal cricket team who played the Melbourne Cricket Club on Boxing Day 1866, captained by Tom Wills

5

He Even Played With the Blacks

There is a second, much inferior photograph of the Australian Native XI taken during their match in Melbourne in Christmas week, 1866. Perhaps because it is too blurred and pale to reveal facial expressions or features it gives a different impression of T.W. Wills. He is on the extreme left, leaning on his bat. The photograph illustrates his lofty physical ease. The previous year, playing with the Geelong club, he was declared Champion of the Colony at Football for the second time. Tom Wills is in his prime. Immediately restored to the captaincy upon his return from New Zealand, he led the Victorian team from the field and through a violent mob in his first match in Sydney, after claims that a New South Wales man had cheated. One Victorian was punched in the incident. 'Scratch a Russian and you will find a Tartar underneath. Scratch a New South Wales man and you discover the evidence of convictism. He may not be a convict himself, but his father was, and it will take many years to obliterate the stain.' *(Melbourne Evening News)*

As ever, there is doubt about the wisdom of Tommy's conduct, but none about his grip on colonial cricket. Two decades later, in the triumphant aftermath of Australia's first Test victory on English soil, an elderly William Tennant will emerge from retirement to write an article seeking to correct reports emanating from England that fast bowler Fred Spofforth is Australia's first 'demon' bowler. That title, says Tennant, correctly belonged to Victoria's Tom Wills. 'He rarely spoke, but batsmen talked about his furious glare.' Wills's philosophy of sport has caused the poet Adam Lindsay Gordon to identify him as a kindred spirit. Gordon, whose Australian nickname is Reckless, has suffered serious head injuries in the course of making his living as a jumps jockey. He believes once you take a line on a jump, the rest is Fate. In a poem in which he mentions Tommy, rhyming Wills with spills, he goes on to say:

> *No game was ever yet worth a rap For a rational man to play,*
> *Into which no accident, no mishap, Could possibly find its way.*

David MacKenzie, Melrose station, 1927

My grandfather, also named David MacKenzie, was much involved in the tour of the Aboriginal cricket team to England in 1868 about which much has been written that is misleading and untrue. Credit for introducing the blacks to the game is given to Mr Charles Lawrence when in fact the Aboriginal team were regularly beating country teams in western Victoria for some years before they met that gentleman. Their early teachers were the sons of families who owned properties in the district, like Tom Hamilton and James Edgar, but my grandfather always believed that the person who influenced them most thereafter, although not connected with them long, was Tom Wills. Grandfather was present the day Wills first encountered the champion Aboriginal batsman Johnny Mullagh.

Mullagh lived for many years beside a waterhole on our property and worked for my grandfather as an odd-job man. He would not have made his living. as a shearer as he regularly recorded the lowest tallies in the shed, but as a rough-horse rider he was without equal. It is said he broke "a horse that had previously thrown seven riders without taking the pipe from between his teeth. As a boy, my father, Lachlan MacKenzie, occasionally played cricket with Johnny Mullagh and some other men behind the woolshed during breaks in work. My father said Mullagh was made to bat with a pick handle because he was impossible to dismiss with anything broader in his hands.

It was men employed by my grandfather who prepared the playing field on the edge of Lake Wallace used for training the Aboriginal team before it left on its tour of England. It was a rough surface but my grandfather, a lover of all sports who once rode a horse to Ballarat to see a prize fight, claimed it provided him with one of the best matches he ever witnessed-Wills against Mullagh. As my father related the story, Wills used every ounce of his strength and guile for over an hour to win the black man's wicket with his' slows', but Mullagh resisted. Eventually, Wills became heated but the quicker he bowled, the more comfortably Mullagh played him (Grandfather said that if Wills had persevered with his spinners, he might have got him, for Mullagh was unable to read slow bowling out of the hand and had to rely on his reflexes once the ball hit the pitch). Finally, Wills did what Grandfather hoped he would do. He produced the delivery that had terrified half the cricketers of Victoria and New South Wales, what is now called a 'bumper' but in those more gentlemanly days was always explained away as an accident caused by slippery fingers. The ball bounced halfway down the pitch and reared at Mullagh's head. As quick as a cat, Mullagh responded with the shot for which he was already famous in the district. He went down on one knee, slanting the bat in front of his face like a shield. Striking the bat, the ball skied over the wicketkeeper's head and hurried away to the long grass on the boundary. At the time, Wills stood in the middle of the pitch, chest heaving, hands on his hips, saying nothing, but afterwards he told Grandfather it was one of the best shots he had seen on a cricket field. Grandfather said the pair never spoke but he observed that when Mullagh developed his bowling he followed Wills's style.

I ask Billy, the Greek kid, if he'd like to come with me on a trip down to the western districts. I tell him I'm doing some research on an old sportsman. He says no thanks. Billy's not interested in sport. He told me once when he was younger that he wanted to be a dancer, but he doesn't talk about that, or much else, any more. His eyes used to have this reckless light. Now they're like used soup bowls, sort of covered over. His mother waves her hands in the air and says she don't know what to do with the boy, and what can I say? The job's gone. We got replaced by ticket machines and there's nothing either of us can do about it. I head west in the old Ford Telstar on my own.

It takes me an hour to get out of the city, driving through the flat expanses of the outer suburbs, past the petrol stations, car yards, fast-food outlets, beyond the new factories that look like white aluminium boxes. The city is imperial. Its outermost colonies, clumps of double-storeyed brick houses in otherwise bare paddocks, are pointed at odd angles to try and make them look individual. Then there's nothing but acres of damp green paddocks and the rough blue line of the mountains to the east. My first feeling, as always, is relief at being away from walls of people. A few hours down the highway, though, other thoughts and feelings will emerge. Shifting, uncertain ones. I grew up out here, surrounded by these low treeless hills. Back then, I would have said there's nothing here. But there is, if you know where to look. In a paddock right beside the highway on the Melbourne side of town is a giant stone eel about 150 paces in length. A farm kid showed it to me when we were at high school. He said it was an eel, but I didn't believe him. Forgot about it, in fact, until I stood in a stone circle in the Outer Hebrides. The lake my home town is built around is full of muddy green eels. The farm kid also had stone tools he had found in his father's paddocks. Thirty miles to the north of the lake, the blue lumps on the horizon are the so-called Grampians. This is Djabwurrung land. Tommy's country.

On an orange boulder a day's ride north of 'Lexington' is a painting of Bunjil, the old man who created this part of the land. With him are two dingoes. At night he can be seen in the heavens, a star with two smaller stars beside him. The story of Bunjil the star I extracted from the diaries of George Augustus Robinson, Protector of Aborigines for the District of Port Phillip, who passed this way in 1841 with a disgruntled man-servant named Mawbey and a train of Aboriginal companions, including a Van Diemen's Land black called Jack. G.A. Robinson was a self-satisfied fool, an upstart bricklayer who went back to England and lacquered his curls to make himself look like Benjamin Disraeli. When the blacks rushed to Robinson, pleading for his protection, he issued them a card bearing his name and that of the Superintendent for the District of Port Phillip, Charles La Trobe-for presentation when attacked under the cover of darkness by men with guns, firing in concert and from protected positions; but he seems to have chronicled his journeys in Port Phillip, and earlier in Van Diemen's Land, faithfully enough. In western Victoria he met squatters claiming runs that were hundreds of square miles. Some would have no blacks on their land. Nearly all had dogs for chasing and killing kangaroos, but if the blacks killed sheep, the whites killed the blacks, or galloped through their camps, scattering the people, driving them away. A few miles north of 'Lexington' an Englishman named Francis invited Robinson in for the night, promising to play him the fiddle. Francis had shot seven blacks. The skull of one of them, placed so that it could be seen, sat a few yards from his front door. One of Robinson's 'sable companions' knew the dead person by name.

To read Robinson's diaries is to know that frontier law is no law at all. Not white law, not black law, just a cycle of revenge and retribution ultimately brought to a halt by the hand that strikes with the most terrifying force. The first reference to Horatio Wills in the diaries suggests the blacks tried to abduct and rape his wife. 'Informed that natives attempted to have connection with Mrs Wills and take her.' One of Horatio Wills's shepherds-a blackguard, according to Robinson-had previously abducted an Aboriginal woman. For everyone white woman in the western districts at that time, there were 10 white men. White men 'treated' openly for black women in Robinson's presence. When Robinson attempted to intervene, a shepherd threatened to punch him in the face and said he would do what he liked with the blacks. H.S. Wills's name subsequently appears in relation to several retributive raids. In one, two women were shot, infants at their breasts. 'God knows there is too much bloodshed in this world!' That's Horatio, two years later, at 'Lexington'. Whole tribes were already extinct, most of them having died of syphilis and smallpox, assisted by the fact that gonorrhoea induced infertility in their womenfolk, but of this he makes no mention in his diaries. Instead, he hyperventilates with religious sentiments and makes worldly pronouncements from afar: 'France and Prussia seem set for war.'

Robinson went to 'Lexington', arriving on a day of heavy rain. He found two huts-one for the overseer and one for the shepherds-and a tent for the family. Standing outside the tent in the downpour, Robinson announced himself in a formal manner. It was some minutes before a white woman with a thin face and startled eyes drew back the canvas flap. Behind her, Robinson could see a small boy aged about six 'with his mother's anxious face'. Mr Wills was away, she said. My party has been five days without meat, declared Robinson. Could I arrange to procure some? Mrs Wills replied abruptly-Yes, in the evening-and closed the canvas flap of the tent. Robinson said 'Lexington' was no place for hungry men to visit. Horatio Wills he never met, but several days down the track he received a written note saying that he wished to speak to him and assist him in his mission. Nine years later, when young Tom Wills embarked for Rugby, the Aboriginal population in Victoria had fallen by 90 per cent-but there were still blacks on 'Lexington'! A young Djabwurrung man appeared at the house asking when Master Tom was coming back. Said the old people wanted to know. 'The blacks had many secrets, particularly the men, but my brother Tom said that when they danced they became creatures of the land.' (Emily Harrison, nee Wills, Melbourne, 1905)

Lake Wallace, now called Edenhope, is 300 miles west of Melbourne, almost on the South Australian border. On an Aboriginal map it belongs to the Jadawardjali, neighbours of the Djabwurrung. Contiguous languages, same totems-Gabadj and Grugidj, the black and the white cockatoo. It is late afternoon when the Ford Telstar and I reach the outskirts of the town. The surrounding country is flat and a dull winter-green in colour, the highway becomes a long main street. Halfway down, as square as a brick, is the town pub. That is my first stop. I get out, body unbending like a bank-note in the cold abrasive air. I push through into the bar, the naked gaze of the few drinkers following me to the counter. They see someone who is not a local but who is also not a threat. It's a trick I learnt on the trams: how to create a neutral presence, how to look like nothing in particular. Which is not what T.W. Wills would have done. How would the drinkers have judged him? In appearance, tall and weathered. Speech terse and to the point, actions instinctive and exact. Eyes? As always, they see without appearing to look but now they also retreat, as a matter of course, from intimacy.

Sarah MacKenzie, Melrose station, Lake Wallace, December 1866

I had looked forward to the entry into my home of a young gentleman from Rugby and Cambridge, cultivated discourse being as rare in these parts as primrose paths, but no inquiry of mine brought a dozen words from his lips. As my husband had informed me he spoke to the blacks in their tongue, I sought to question him on this when we were seated at the table for our evening meal, saying, 'Surely the purpose of the game is that it is a means of teaching them a civilized language.'

The question appeared to unsettle him and he replied, 'The game is civilized, is it not?', whereupon my husband, who is lost in any but the coarsest company, bellowed, 'Bravo, Wills!', and the moment was lost.

I will allow that he displayed kindness to our son. Lachlan had talked of nothing but Mr Wills for the month before his arrival. As a small child, he displayed a lively intelligence which I hoped to see harnessed into the study of the natural sciences at one of the great universities of England, but now all he reads and talks about are events depicted in the sporting press. The boy was agog with excitement when Mr. Wills arrived and was received by him in a kindly manner. He even asked Lachlan if he would care to join him for a practice before tea. I must confess I watched from the scullery, the small boy racing about, a windmill of arms and legs, the man moving to retrieve the ball in a leisurely, practised sort of way. At one point, I saw him stop and arrange Lachlan's way of holding the bat, teaching him to move in a way both forward and back. They played easily and well for over an hour. Lachlan strode back to the house, cheeks flushed with pleasure. I naturally assumed something of that good feeling would transfer back into my house, but no, on passing through the door, Mr Wills was once again his former cold self. He ate joylessly, like a parson, and as soon as dinner was concluded excused himself, saying he had business in Lake Wallace. It was after midnight that I awoke to the blurred, heavy sound of a drunk entering my house.

Do a quick tour of the town, fixing its symbols in my mind. To the left of the main road is a small bluestone Presbyterian church dedicated to the area's Scottish pioneers. One block to the right, Lake Wallace - a vast silver-grey sheet of wrinkled water. Above it, the overcast sky has the muted lustre of sunset. Darkness is one hour away, at most two. I seek out the playing field where Tom Wills first met Johnny Mullagh. It's a schoolyard now. A man on an orange tractor is giving it a regulation cut, a fine green spray arcing from his spinning blades. Behind him is a yellow weatherboard school with white windows and a silver corrugated-iron roof. A stone cairn commemorating the Aboriginal team stands in the foreground, but when all is said and done it looks like a schoolyard. Drive on, find the local showgrounds on the other side of the main street with a line of tall dark pines. Beneath them, a cluster of wooden sheds briefly shine silver-grey in the late evening light.

Circling the arena is a series of low stools fashioned from stumps and planks, the sort of seating to be found at the MCG in Tommy's day. Get out of the car and walk towards the centre of the showgrounds, long wet grass whipping my ankles, and picture Tommy meeting the Aboriginal players for the first time, the young officer talking to them in Djabwurrung, about cricket, them with one eye on him, one on the horizon, listening without appearing to. One of the Aboriginal cricketers, Harry Rose was a forebear of Lionel Rose, world bantamweight champion in the late '60s. Lionel Rose was one of the heroes of my youth. I watched his fights on TV and felt every blow. One of his defences was against an Englishman, Alan Rudkin. Rudkin was brave but artless, forever advancing. Rose let him, relying on his reflexes to evade him in close and score with counter-punches. Rose's cousin, a Gunditjmara man named Reg Saunders, was the first Aborigine to be commissioned as an officer in the Australian Army. In the *Age,* on Anzac Day 1989, Reg Saunders said his people fought a classic guerilla war, in western Victoria, attacking the enemy's food supplies, destroying his crops and livestock; but, in military terms, they had two disadvantages they couldn't overcome. The first was weaponry. The second was the fact that they couldn't protect their women and children.

The war was particularly fierce in Jadawardjali country. It is remembered in names like the Fighting Hills and the Fighting Waterholes. The Native Police, under the command of Captain Dana, shot 20 blacks in a single engagement on Konongwootong Creek. Captain Dana was the first member of the Melbourne Club to die in his bed on club premises. Victoria is no different from Queensland or Tasmania, not in its roots. What differs are the attitudes layered over the events. Tasmania's shame is public and well known. It had a Black War. Victoria didn't. It had the Native Police who were trained by Captain Dana to work in a thoroughly Victorian way. 'The members of the (Port Phillip Native Police) Force will not only be taught to consider themselves superior to other blacks, but also to discriminate between the various classes of whites.'

I go back to the lake for the last of the light, immediately seeing what I missed at first sight - the birdlife. Herons, white-fronted cranes, black swans, moor hens, ducks, white cockatoos. A dirt track leads towards the lake's western edge. I take it, eventually stopping in front of a colony of elderly red gums with great wrinkly guts and vulgar belly buttons and massive tangled crowns. One has a branch that has sought to escape and start a tree of its own, running along the ground for about 30 paces, then making a vertical ascent and sprouting leaves, The light is a grey veil now with black at its edges. I open the car door. Startled, a flock of small ducks sitting nearby lift into the air, beating their wings on the water. Not for the first time, I wonder if I really want to go on. Who knows what awaits us in the dark? Tommy certainly didn't. He thought war was a game, Evans House against School-house with a mug of beer and a song around the fire when it was done. Then he came back and was confronted with the reality, bodies rotting in the sun like the carcasses of sheep, infants clubbed to death, women and children running from men on horses with repeating rifles. The whole impossible bloody mess. If I ever had a choice, it's one I made a long time ago when I decided this place was home. I stumble forward, the shifting black surface of the lake appearing beneath me. A sudden ecstasy of coldness in my shoes tells me I am standing in water. Shivering now, I expose myself to the night.

T.W.W. to Emily Harrison (nee Wills), Lake Wallace, 12 December 1866

> . . . the only people with whom one can pass a tolerable evening are the shepherds and they are unspeakably dim after years of standing on hilltops & talking to sheep. They talk about the war that was fought around here no-one else does so unlike Queensland where everyone boasts of killing blacks the lake is pretty at night & sometimes I walk there . . .

Depart Edenhope by Harrow road. Take the lesser road where it forks at the edge of town. No need to speed. Poodle past wet paddocks fringed with gums and paperbarks and clumps of dirty-coloured sheep, map on my knee. For breakfast an orange juice, its sweet astringent strength something for the guts to cling on to. Drank too much last night. Again. Woke feeling poisoned, mouth like a sodden carpet. After thirty minutes, an old white homestead with a large shearing shed appears on the right. Immediately past it, on the left, a sand track leads into virgin bush. The road to Johnny Mullagh's waterhole. Leaving the road the car dips, the track narrows and bush crowds around. I put down the window and let in air. The smell combines the fragrance of native flora with the industry of ants. Honeysuckle trees, kangaroo-tail bushes, white and pink heath, spiky native grasses, dead limbs of trees all interwoven. Old MacKenzie used to ride through here on his horse to cajole Johnny into playing for Harrow. That was in Johnny's later years. Old MacKenzie would sit in his trap on the edge of the Harrow ground and signal when the necessary runs had been scored. Johnny would duly depart next ball, conveniently caught at slip or wherever else he deemed appropriate, and receive rations and the odd pound note for his services.

Mullagh, Johnny. Date of birth unknown, thought to have been about 25 during the tour of England. In the photograph of the Australian Native XI taken at the Melbourne Cricket Ground on Boxing Day 1866, he stands to the immediate right of Wills, face inscrutable. Four months later, in the course of

an athletic program, Mullagh recorded the highest jump seen in the colony -
5 feet 4 inches. Officials said he would have leapt higher had the ground not
been wet. The outstanding player on the 1868 tour. Played in 45 of the 47
matches, taking 257 wickets and scoring 1698 runs. When the Australians, as
they are recorded in Wisden, played the gentlemen of the Marylebone
Cricket Club at Lord's and led by 21 runs on the first innings, Mullagh had -
at that stage of the match scored 75 of his team's total of 186 and taken five
wickets for 82 runs. Then Bullocky somehow went missing and the visitors
collapsed to lose the match after being in a winning position. Upon
their return from England Mullagh was hired by the Melbourne Cricket Club
as a professional, but, unable to settle in the city, returned to western
Victoria, thereafter playing for Harrow. Recalled to the Victorian XI to
play Lord Harris's Englishmen at the age of 40, he top-scored with
36 in the second innings. 'His long reach, his cool artistic drives and
his judicious treatment of dubious balls called forth loud applause.'

Died 1891. At his funeral, many fine words spoken.

Mullagh was humble, upright and civil; a noble type of an almost extinct
race. A contemporary painting makes him look like another Imperial exotic,
the Indian cricketer Ranjitshinji. Being neither Catholic nor Protestant,
Mullagh was buried with the paupers but his gravestone, paid for by the
Harrow Cricket Club, is one of the biggest in the cemetery. It reads, 'Johnny
Mullagh, Champion Aboriginal Cricketer.' Mullagh is still a name in those
parts. The local caravan park is named after him. An urn bearing his image
stands beside the Harrow footy oval. When I saw the ground, sheep were
grazing on its hard, bumpy surface. Johnny Mullagh must be just about the
first black hero in white Australian history. Why? Could it be, as I have read,
connected to the secession movement then brewing in the western districts of
Victoria? Proposed name for the new colony: Princeland. The mythology fits
in a shadowy sort of way. Johnny's death certificate gives his father's name as
King Watertight. But there were no kings or chiefs among the blacks; William
Buckley told them that.

Old MacKenzie gave Johnny Mullagh a silver watch and chain which he
wore but never set or wound. Old MacKenzie noticed that whenever he and
Johnny were discussing a forthcoming match, Johnny would always
conclude the business by saying, 'What day yesterday?' Then he would ask,
'What day tomorrow?' But he never asked what day it was today, any more
than he had ever asked what time it was now. Johnny kept his own time. He
was a proud man. In York, the Aboriginal players were refused admission to
the refreshment tent during the lunch break. When play resumed, Mullagh
refused to take the field. In later years, when he was playing for Harrow
against nearby Apsley, the captain of the opposition team whispered 'Nigger'

to him when he was batting. Next ball, Mullagh hit him an obvious catch and walked from the field. The game was over. The Apsley captain had killed it as surely as a wanton boy with a gun can kill a bird. Who knows? Johnny might have said it wasn't cricket. He was once asked why he never married. He replied, 'Because a white woman would never have me, and I'd never have a black one.' Or so the story goes in white folklore. They say Johnny lived by his waterhole alone but for his dogs and the daguerreotype of some gentlewomen he met in England. True? Perhaps. Remember Othello.

The bush becomes less tangled, the track flatter and more open. Enter a clearing. This is it, a waterhole edged with four red gums, some five or six hundred years old. They look like ancient castles with sticks sprouting at odd angles from their turrets. The black water is ringed with white sand; there are ducks among the rushes. I get out of the car, take a few steps and mutter my apology. The truth is I don't even know his name. Early records list him not as Johnny Mullagh but Mullagh Johnny. Mullagh was the station he worked on. Before that he was Black Johnny, which is hardly a name at all, merely a description. The *London Sporting Life* of 16 May 1868 gives his real name as Unaarrimin. Try to say it, to work it into a sound like the shudder of a spear. I can't. And who spelt the word anyway, who apportioned it those sounds in English? He certainly didn't. I'm entering a mental labyrinth from which there is no exit, one I have previously spent hours trapped in, when I hear a loud shriek of laughter raining down from the heavens. A black cockatoo. I laugh *too,* and thank him for his advice.

Emily Harrison, nee Wills, to her cousin Jane Harrison, 1867

After the second baby died, Coley was three days from work. On the third morning, he received a curt note from Mr Tyler, the head of the Customs Department in Melbourne, asking why he had been absent without explanation. I said he should write, 'What-you would think me a better man if I attended work and missed my daughter's funeral!', but Coley said it would be a foolish impertinence.

Disembarking at Queen Street pier after a journey of eight days, the Aboriginal cricketers arrive with Tommy's last hope and find themselves in a dark, sprawling growth said to rival Naples for stench. Most houses have open cesspits, and the waste from animals kept in backyards-pigs, ducks, fowls, cows, horseswashes into the city's gutters and drains. The water from the much-vaunted reservoir at Yan Yean is limited in quantity and mawkish, and 1500 deaths each year are attributed to 'filth' diseases like typhoid. Half the deaths are of children below the age of five. The Gold Rush has been followed by drought and depression, and the only money being made is through speculation. Crime has increased, the flasher thieves basing themselves in the fag end of the Chinese quarter in Little Bourke Street, or Collingwood. The slums at the end of Little Lonsdale Street are compared to Spitafields in London for squalor and overcrowding. The homeless sleep along the banks of the river, beneath Prince's Bridge and on the wharf. Enlisting to fight in the Maori wars in New Zealand, one recruit gives his address as 'the third gas-pipe on Cole's wharf'. This expression passes into the vernacular, meaning nowhere to go. The Gold Rush has bequeathed to Victoria a generation of children conceived in a mood of reckless optimism, many of whom have then been abandoned. On the second day of the Australian Native XI's match at the MCG, an Irish Catholic and former Van Diemen's Land convict named Red Kelly dies from dropsy in a slab hut thirty miles north of Melbourne, a recent stint in prison for stealing a calf at the height of the drought having broken his health. His death makes 12-year-old Edward, also known as Ned, the man of the house.

The colony's politics are now openly divided. The large radical group in the Legislative Assembly has brought the democratic temper of the Gold Rush into direct conflict with the established interests of the colony as represented by the Legislative Council. The result is a deadlock between the two houses of parliament. When the Governor, Sir Charles Darling, sides with the popularly elected lower house, the forces aligned against him engineer his recall to London. The *Age,* which backed the miners in the uprising at Ballarat 12 years earlier, has sided with the Legislative Assembly. 'It is difficult to estimate how great the number was before the Governor's farewell procession started, but all Melbourne seemed to have turned out. The most noticeable feature of the whole gathering was its quietness.' As Sir Charles's carriage passes the Melbourne Club and the offices of the *Argus,* hissing is heard, 'this being an example of the good taste for which the snob is proverbial.' The previous year, at the height of the American Civil War, the Melbourne Club had thrown open its doors to the officers of the Confederate warship *Shenandoah,* a steam sloop which had been plundering American shipping in the Pacific and had docked in Melbourne for supplies of coal and repairs. 'No doubt the soft-headed flunkeys who are the leaders of the Melbourne· Club think slavery a "mighty fine" institution, too.' Again, the *Age.*

Those who can afford to do so have begun pushing south of the river. Where a child was lost in the bush ten years ago is now a suburb called Hawthorn. While not as spacious or grand as neighbouring Kew, it has clean air and mostly brick houses that sit on their own block of land. Further south, the beachside suburb of St Kilda is dotted with mansions belonging to successful speculators and retired squatters, many of which, in imitation of Government House, erect square towers from which their owners can enjoy a clear view of Port Phillip Bay extending all the way to the faint outline of its heads. Melbourne is spreading along the bay. It is amid the tea-tree and light scrub at nearby Brighton beach that the body of poet Adam Lindsay Gordon will be found in four years' time, his skull shattered by the rifle held between his knees, pipe and tobacco neatly placed beside him in his hat. William Tennant, who has dealt with Gordon in his capacity as the sporting editor of the *Australasian*, will describe his death as 'perhaps inevitable'.

From the *Australasian*, 2 January 1866 by 'Fine Leg' (William Tennant)

There is no doubt that at cricket the blacks are a failure, as with the exception of Mullagh, Cuzens and Bullocky, they do not play well enough to create a genuine interest. Last weekend's match, grandly billed as the meeting of the Australian Native XI with a Rest of the World XI, was scheduled to last four days. In the event, it collapsed in one, only Mullagh producing a sustained performance with the bat, scoring 16 of the Aboriginal Eleven's 39 runs in the first innings, and 33 from a total of 87 in the second (T.W. Wills 25 not out). A second match produced a similarly calamitous result and, in an effort to recoup costs, a program of athletics events had to be organised. At these, the blacks showed themselves to considerable advantage. Tarpot was very near to Barrass in the hop, step and jump which is saying a good deal for him, as we think, if pressed, Barrass could do 45 ft. In the 100 yards, Tarpot and Dick-a-Dick defeated Maude, who competed for colonial championship honours, but at long distance races they are evidently 'no good'. Throwing the spear was a failure, the spears being bad; and the boomerang throwing was hardly satisfactory either, though Dick-a-Dick and Mullagh performed with that peculiar instrument a good many times, but the boomerangs were evidently not first quality. Their eccentric flights through the air puzzled and amused the spectators immensely.

Introducing Tommy's nemesis - William Josiah Tennant. Sallow face, slightly built, soft brown eyes, small neat moustache. Arrived Melbourne mid-1850s, having played cricket for Cambridge and the Gentlemen of Surrey. Described thus in the 1859 Victorian Cricketers' Guide by J.B. Ellis (a fellow student at Trinity College)-'Has a fine forward wristy style of play, and hits the ball beautifully to square leg. Having had but little practice the last season is not the pink of bats he was upon arriving from England, but a very good ball, unless an off bailer, will seldom take his wicket. Bowls straight with a peculiar delivery, shifting the ball from one hand to the other at the last moment. Requires careful playing & is particularly destructive to tyros. Can field well at slip, but is not fond of too much running or throwing.' In short, not the sort of cricketer much respected by T.W. Wills. 'The demands he made of himself and others only increased with the years and many a younger player chose to continue with a bruised calf or aching joint rather than report an injury to Tommy Wills.' (Alfred Bonicelli, 'Spectator' of the *Melbourne Illustrated News*)

Tennant was Tommy's predecessor as Captain of the Victorian XI. 'Wills played surprisingly poorly in his first Grand Intercolonial.' Did Tommy white-ant Tennant? Possibly. He was only ever interested in running the show. Along with Wills and J.B. Ellis, Tennant was also a member of the Melbourne Cricket Club sub-committee which drew up the first rules for the Game of Football in May 1859. In 1862, Tennant began writing for the *Australasian*, the *Argus's* weekly paper, under the nom-de-plume 'Fine Leg'. This probably coincides with the date of of his retirement as a player. By the mid-1870s, he was the newspaper's sports editor. Judging from the tone of Tennant's early articles, he and Wills were originally friends, or perhaps it is more accurate to say that Tennant thought they were, a certain complacency being evident in a number of his judgments, not least his decision to publicly mock T.W.W.'s use of language after a letter of resignation with his signature affixed appeared in the sporting press beneath the following piece of classical wisdom: *Nevermore; vae victis*. 'In his now famous (or should we say foolish?) letter, T.W.W. managed to present himself as a previously unknown collision between Livy, the Roman scholar of antiquity, and Mr Edgar Allan Poe, the American poet of our time!' Without doubt, the best line written about T.W. Wills in his lifetime, the suggestion being that he carried the thoroughly modern madness of Poe within the formal structure of Livy, but did Tennant know it? Probably not. The world, at the time of which we speak, was pre-Freud. Psyche was still a maid standing beside a pool of still water. Discussions of human motivation were usually restricted to the old Biblical duality of good and evil. Take, for instance, the case of Mr Sherlock Holmes. What is interesting about the great 19th century detective is that he asks no questions of himself. He has no interest in women ('the fair sex, Watson, are your department'), about as much in art, merely playing the violin in abstract fashion when musing upon a case; he's a keen amateur boxer - the best, pound for pound, that Watson had seen - but, between cases, when there is nothing in the papers he uses cocaine 'as a protest against the monotony of existence'. Holmes is addicted to action. He has no other way of engaging the world. Like, I suspect, T.W. Wills.

From the *Sydney Sporting Life,* **4 May 1867**
ABORIGINALS V. ELEVEN OF NEW SOUTH WALES

The engagement with the blacks to tour England having fallen through, it was decided to play a match, which took place last Monday and Tuesday, for the sole purpose of defraying the expense of getting them back to their home, viz., Lake Wallace in Victoria. With this view, the Albert 'company allowed them the use of their ground for both days above mentioned. I must say the Aborigines have improved wonderfully since I saw them last, which I attribute to the fact that they have been coached by Englishman Mr Charles Lawrence and marshalled by that truly acknowledged warrior chieftain Mr T.W. Wills who has been untiring in his efforts to bring them well disciplined and competent before the public. In fact, the Native XI bears his stamp in more than one respect as' even the least recognised of their batsmen stand unflinching before the fast ball.

From the *Geelong Advertiser,* **'The Sports', 11 May 1867**

The Native Eleven played against eleven of the Corio club last Friday and Saturday, beating them easily in one innings. Mullagh again got the highest score for the natives (45 of 180) but decidedly more interest was felt in the sports which came off after the match, the ground being lined with visitors in carriages, on horseback, and on foot, all of whom were anxious to witness the wonderful powers of the blacks in jumping, of which so much has been written and said. Before entering into an account of the various events we must not forget to thank the managing committee, Messrs. Nicholls, Buckland, Hayman and Wills, who were indefatigable in their exertions to make the sports pass off successfully. The police, under the command of Sergeant McSweeney, were there if wanted, but, unlike the recent scenes at the ground of the Melbourne club, their services were not called into requisition. The first event was the
150 YARDS HANDICAP FLAT RACE
J. Cuzens, 3 yards. 1
Jellico, 5 yards. 2
F. Carr, 3 yards. 3
    Fourteen entries in all: time 17 secs, against a strong wind.

THROWING CRICKET BALL
Bullocky, 109 yd. 2 ft. 9 in.
Mullagh, 106 yd. 1 ft. 3 in.
Cuzens, 104 yd. 1 ft.

This was thrown across the wind. There were eight entries, but only seven came to the post. Rippon was the only one who came anywhere near the natives, he in his first attempt throwing 101 yards.

100 YARDS FLAT RACE
E. Nicholls, 1
Tarpot, 2
Cuzens, 3

There was immense excitement about this race, for which there were six entries, it being known that Nicholls (the crack of Geelong) and Tarpot (the pet of Lake Wallace) were to meet on equal terms. A good start was effected, Nicholls having, if anything, the best of it. He led all the way, Tarpot almost abreast of him. Time 11 secs.

RUNNING HOP, STEP, AND JUMP
Tarpot, 39 ft. 6 in.
W. Irwin, 39 ft.

440 YARDS HANDICAP FLAT RACE
Jellico, 8 yards 1
F. Carr, scratch 2

Four started, Carr being the favourite. Jellico, however, held his own, winning by four yards. Time 51 secs.

CRICKETERS' HANDICAP FLAT RACE-200 YARDS
Bullocky, 1
Cuzens, 2

STANDING HIGH JUMP
Tarpot, Cuzens and Mullagh tied at 4ft 3^1/2 in. Great amusement was occasioned by little Cuzens who jumped nearly his own height. Diamond, a white man, cleared four feet and half an inch.

300 YARDS HANDICAP HURDLE RACE
M. Fox, scratch 1
Tarpot, 3 yards 2

There were ten entries. Tarpot, who came in two or three yards behind the leader, fell over one of the competitors during the race. Time 47 secs.

100 YARDS BACKWARDS

Tarpot, 1

Bowden, 2

The manner in which Tarpot went away from his opponents was wonderful to see. He won by a score of yards in 14 secs, The band then played 'God Save The Queen'. Three cheers were given for the Victorian Eleven, three for the Corio club, and the amusements terminated.

The *Australasian*, 1 July 1867, by 'Fine Leg' (William Tennant)

It has always been my opinion that the publicity meted out to the Aboriginal cricketers was - with the exception of the batting of Mullagh and the bowling of Cuzens - out of proportion to their abilities, and that the notion of taking the team to England and matching them against county sides runs the risk of serious embarrassment, both sporting and financial. The principal enjoyment afforded by the team is in the performance of novelty sports but on the last occasion the blacks appeared in Melbourne, the mob was most unruly, the police gave every appearance of being powerless, and the fence surrounding the M.C.C. pavilion was in danger of being destroyed by the pressure of the crowd. On this account the most interesting feature of the program, dodging the cricket ball with the shield and leawell, was a failure, Dick-a-Dick, who is a splendid specimen of a darkie, being placed at a considerable disadvantage from so many pressing close behind the throwers.

The blacks are a civil, well-behaved set of men and I am told that Dick-a-Dick, Jellico and Tarpot are brothers. Dick-a-Dick in particular is a fine fellow and would make a good secretary, so I am told, to a Temperance Society, for it will delight all total abstainers who believe all blackfellows are powerless before the temptation of intoxicating liquor to know that this darky has a horror of drunkenness and visits any of his brothers who indulge in the vice, indeed any member of the team, with condign punishment; I am told he can lay it on strong, and does so. Jellico is also a most agreeable young fellow who amused many with his quick wit. He drew loud laughter in the MCC pavilion during the lunch-break on the first day when he was asked if Mr Wills was teaching the Aboriginals in his care to read and write. 'Wills no use,' responded the young man brightly. 'He along us. He talk blackfellah language.'

The agreement whereby the darkies, Mr Wills and others in the party were bound hand and foot to the gentleman who initially proposed the tour of England, Edward Brougham Gurnett Esquire, is a model one that would puzzle a Philadelphia lawyer. It is a pity that gentleman who drew it up and the honourable Mr Gurnett cannot pay a visit to Lake Wallace. The blacks would be glad to see them, I know, and dance a corroboree in their honour. They may also initiate them into the mysteries of using the waddy or the leawell, the latter a most formidable weapon that would raise a nasty lump on any cranium. It was indeed a most unfortunate day for the blacks when that agreement was signed. Had they proceeded to New South Wales on their own hook (and not been hooked by a Gurnett) they would each have realised a handsome little sum of money, and Mr Wills would not have given up all his time and .trouble for nought. That being so, I must admit to being somewhat puzzled to find his feelings so injured by the fact that this new plan to take the team to England excludes him, unless the reason be that after a career as illustrious as his, he would like to cap it off by being presented to Royalty which may well occur if the blacks are given a fixture at Lord's...

No doubt about it, that would have been the crowning moment of his career, presented to Royalty at Lord's, along with Red Cap and Dick-a-Dick and Bullocky, but most of all with Mullagh, his one true peer, even if the injury that lay between them was too deep for words. So why didn't he go? A couple of reasons. Tommy and Charles Lawrence hadn't got on during the earlier tour; both no doubt wanted to be in command. Lawrence has been described as the smarter politician, but that wouldn't be hard. Tom Wills had the political skills of a goat. That's where the word tragedy comes from, so I have read. From the Greek words *tragos,* meaning goat; and *oide,* song of. And, by this time, more than sporting pride, more even than money, was being invested in the tour. The old Victorian double standard was being wheeled into play: 'In cricket, with its requirements of agility, nerve, self-possession, obedience to law, we see the savage put in contact with a superior race under the healthiest conditions practicable. The order of civilisation in the Christian sense seems to be to first make savages men and then to make them Christians.' *(Ballarat Star)* The *Age* meantime had urged its readers to help smooth the pillow of a dying race and there was now a fear that should the blacks be exposed to alcohol on the tour a number would die. The issue of whether they should be permitted to even leave the colony was being vigorously debated in the pages of the major newspapers. All that is needed in such cases is a word in the right ear.

From a letter by Trooper Kennedy at Lake Wallace to the secretary of the Board for the Protection of Aborigines in Victoria, 13 June 1867

Of the Aboriginal cricketers that left Lake Wallace eight months ago to play in Melbourne and Sydney, four are now dead. The native known as 'Sugar' died before the first game, while 'Watty' passed away in the cart on the way home some twenty miles from Lake Wallace. Since their return, two more, 'Jellico' and 'Paddy', have also passed on. In each case, the cause of death has been given as pneumonia or discharge of the lungs, but evidence tendered at the post-mortem of the native 'Watty' at the Lake Wallace Hotel on May 27 inst., conducted by Doctor Fisher from Portland, revealed that the deceased, as well as others of the team, were continually drunk on the tour. In this respect, I am obliged to remark upon the behaviour of the team captain, Mr T.W. Wills. Prior to departing, the blacks were in the habit of firing a tree on the western side of the lake at night. More than once, Mr Wills was observed in their circle, rum bottle in hand. When I approached Mr Wills and advised him on the correct way to handle the blacks, he laughed wildly and said he had just seen a ghost.

6

The Final Act

From *Adventures in Colonial Portraiture*
by William Fraser MacDonald, Auckland, 1885

In pursuance of my long-held belief that setting often provides a significant clue as to character, I had written to Mr W- inviting him to choose the time and place for a preliminary sketch. His reply, expressed in a neat, well-ordered hand, asked that I meet him at the Melbourne Cricket Ground at five o'clock the following evening. This, frankly, was a disappointment. On match days, the Melbourne Cricket Ground is decorated with tents and marquees and, given what I had been told about Mr W-'s reticent nature, I had counted on the carnival atmosphere lending animation to his features. Instead, I arrived at the ground at the appointed time to find its emptiness emphasised by the vacant benches of a magnificent newly erected grandstand designed to provide seating for several hundred. A young groundsman, seeing my sketch-books and inquiring as to my purpose, volunteered to locate Mr W- and disappeared into a small wooden pavilion between the grandstand and the scoreboard.

As is my practice, I had sought information about my subject before meeting him, which in this case had not been at all difficult as Mr T-WW-, Victoria's most famous cricketer, was freely spoken about by people of all classes. Indeed, Mr W- had the dubious distinction of being the first gentleman cricketer in the colony to be on first-name terms with the mob. On match days, they would lean over the fence and call out to him in a familiar way (to them, he was 'T-y W-s'). According to some, his status with the 'larrikins', as the hooligan element in that colony is known, was based on the fact that he drank even more than they did, although all parties were anxious to affirm that he was never drunk on match days.

To be frank, it was not a commission I approached with much eagerness. The previous year, Mr W- had walked from the field as a match against the neighbouring colony of New South Wales was about to begin because another had been chosen in preference to him as captain of the Victorian Eleven. This is a gentleman's prerogative, I was told, but not a professional's, even as in this case where there is no disputing that the professional is the best man for the job. It was even rumoured that bailiffs had visited Mr W- in the Victorian team's dressing room during a Grand Inter-Colonial match in Sydney on account of an unpaid debt from an earlier visit to that city.

My expectation was that I would be met by a blunt, hard-faced man in whites. To my considerable surprise, the figure which emerged from the pavilion and proceeded towards me in a manner I can only describe as stately looked like some pasha of the East. He was wearing a bow tie, a brocaded cap, two-tone shoes, and, strapped around his midriff, a brightly coloured sash; in his right hand, he carried a bat in the manner of a walking cane. When he was almost upon me, the young groundsman who had fetched him cried out, 'Show him your best side, T-. Hide your belly.' This astonishing gust of vulgarity met with a faint ripple of mirth from the great man who nonetheless did not deem it worth a turning of his head. Instead, we shook hands, exchanging gruff pleasantries, and, for one instant, I felt his gaze pass through me like a shadow that stretched to the depth of my being. Then, apparently not having found what he sought, his eyes swept away to settle on the slope opposite, above the playing field.

The moment that follows the first introduction is the most fraught for the portraitist. This is when both parties must lower themselves into the small, unstable craft of conversation. Mr W- dispensed with this problem with, it must be conceded, considerable style. Having presented his profile in the manner of a Caesar submitting to a sculptor preparing his bust, he no longer seemed to care, or indeed know (I had smelt claret on his breath when we exchanged our handshake), that I was present. That being the case, I took the opportunity to study my subject in detail. In build, he was powerful but possessed of a waist. He had a drinker's face with burst capillaries in the nose and upper cheeks, and great pale eyes that observed the world steadily and without emotion. Overall, he looked older than his age, given to me as thirty-five years, and his costume, so grand at first sight, was yellowed and stained.

'May I compliment you on the setting, Mr Wills,' I said. The Melbourne Cricket Ground is built in a shallow cup of land above the Yarra River. It is surrounded by eucalypts, an untidy shapeless tree to be found like a weed across the length and breadth of the continent. I went on, 'The evening light adds an Olympian quality to the playing field.'

'Yes,' he said.

I had been warned that he was no conversationalist. 'It's important I get this right,' I said, beginning to sketch. 'How I portray you may determine the manner in which you are seen by future generations.' Flattery is as indispensable to my trade as a hammer and nail is to a carpenter.

'A New Zealander?' he replied, turning briefly in my direction.

'Yes. I left Christchurch three years ago.' There was a moment's silence, then he said, 'I went to New Zealand in '63. I met ship farmers in New Zelland,' the last statement being uttered in imitation of my accent. A smile lingered stupidly on his face. During my five years in the colony, this tedious joke, or an obscene relation of it, was made at my expense almost on a daily basis. Of course, such sentiments merely declare the provincialism of the mind from whom they proceed, but as this one had arisen in the course of a commission I said nothing (as I have told my students many times, ours is a furtive art). Instead, I asked him why he had gone to New Zealand.

'Why?' He frowned. 'To play cricket, of course.'

'Where were you before you went to New Zealand?'

'Queensland.'

For the first time since I had begun drawing, he looked at me direct. 'Have you been to Queensland?' I had to say that I had not. He looked away. 'People think Melbourne is hot in February. Queensland is an oven. A man's skin bakes like clay.'

'How ghastly,' I said, seeking to confirm him in the direction of his thinking and thereby relax him, but my remark seemed immediately to incline him to the contrary view. .

'Ghastly?' he said. 'Not at all. Have you ever seen a brolga? They have wings like the sleeves of a grey cardigan.' To my surprise, he began using his arms to imitate a bird in flight. 'No,' he went on. 'Queensland is paradise-that's why there are so many snakes there.' He laughed at this remark, a strange, discordant sound.

'Were you on your own up there?' I asked.

He thought before replying, 'No,' but then was more silent than before. Again his attention was directed to the slope on the opposite side of the playing field. The setting sun was in the gum trees, making even the dead branches glow. The thought occurred to me that perhaps Mr T- W- W belonged in this mad, tangled place. He was lordly, but in a casual way. He stood like the 'bush' youth did, with a kind of studied insolence, one foot crossed in front of the other, leaning on his bat.

'How grand a game is cricket?' I asked, again seeking to draw him forth. 'Very grand,' he replied. 'Anyone can play.' The Victorian Cricket Association had presented me with a weighty task. They required a portrait of their longest serving captain that would be the equal of any in the great pavilions and club-houses of England. Here was a man educated at the famous Rugby school and Cambridge university, but to date I knew as much about him as a house one passes from the street. In a moment of desperation, I asked a preposterous question, one I would have otherwise thought fit only for a child, to wit - 'Who is the best cricketer in the world?'

'I am,' he replied. Even with my lack of knowledge on the subject, I found his certainty mildly shocking. I rephrased my question as gracefully as any barrister. 'Who is the best cricketer other than yourself?'

'Grace. But I haven't see him play. He hadn't begun when I left England, but one reads enough about him. The Great W.G. I look forward to meeting him one day.'

'On the field?'

'Of course.'

And, with that, I had him! T-y W-s was a stance. My mistake had been to seek a philosophy. Having achieved a certain impression, my mind immediately proceeded to the question of an appropriate backdrop, and I resolved to place him in front of something dark and formal like a line of firs.

Tommy asks Ced to be consulted about Cullin-la-ringo 'as naturally it is a matter of some consequence to me, as I know it is to you.' He says these are the questions to be asked if it is to be sold. How many sheep can it run? What are the water reserves? How many can it carry in a dry season? He himself is thinking of moving to Fiji. 'Cotton growing pays well and labour costs but very little. The climate I am told by many is most healthy & salubrious - quite a number are going from here - and with care a person would I feel confident do well in a few years.' He has heard what is being said in Geelong, that there were no more sheep on Cullin-la-ringo when he left than when Father arrived. 'I have told Mother there is no point the trustees seeking to shake my hand if I meet them in the street.'

Fiji never eventuates. He is in debt. 'Everything is very dull here.' What has Tommy other than games? Nothing. There is nothing between the games but a silence as large and haunted as the land he stands in. Tommy clings on, becoming notorious for his ruses.

Melbourne Cricket Ground, Richmond versus Melbourne, December 1871, small crowd in. Veteran bowler T.W. Wills tells the umpire he is concerned that he might be overstepping the crease with his delivery stride. He indicates the technical nature of the problem, thrusting the left foot forward, simultaneously bringing the right arm around, and says, 'I fear no-balling.' The umpire agrees to assist by scrutinising the placement of Tommy's feet on the next delivery. With the eyes of officialdom directed downwards, Tommy raises his bowling arm and lets rip with a throw that shatters the batsman's stumps. Howls of indignation and outrage from the members' pavilion, a look of mock innocence on Tommy's face, laughter from the larrikins on the fence. *Old Tommy's done 'em again.*

Football is now the popular game. The Grand Inter-colonials have lost their lustre and Test cricket is yet to be invented. Football is played in public parks and there is no admission fee. Games between Melbourne and Carlton, played on 'the gravel pit' outside the Melbourne Cricket Ground, now draw crowds of 10000 people. There is no members' reserve and no special area for the ladies, all mix as one: squatters, selectors, barristers, barmaids, women of the night, factory boys, Catholics, Protestants, members of parliament and the 'pushes': that is, the larrikins who follow their local clubs. The larrikins do not have their parents' fear of authority. They dress loudly - 'flash' is the term - wearing trousers that fit like stockings and high-heeled boots. They spit tobacco juice wherever they choose and stone the opposition team's carriage with blue metal if they are displeased with the result of a game. In the words of one of their number, nineteen-year-old Ned Kelly from Greta, in Victoria's far north-east, he and his friends aim to live bold, fearless and free. A Flogging Act is being talked about to control them. Others suggest organised sports like cricket and football.

Colden Harrison, retired as a player but five times Champion of the Colony at Football, petitions the Melbourne City Council to have some of the red gums removed from the footballers' playing field on the slope above the Melbourne Cricket Ground. He supports his plea with a reminder of the game's character, which he describes as British and manly. It is Harrison, in his capacity as a member of the committee of the Melbourne Cricket Club, who successfully broaches the subject of football actually being played on the cricket ground. The resultant fixture, played for the benefit of the Children's Hospital, leaves scrapes and cuts on the surface of the playing field. 'Harrison, you have ruined our ground!' It is another ten years before footballers, again at Colden Harrison's discreet prompting, are allowed back onto the MCG.

Tommy keeps playing with Geelong, becoming Champion of the Colony for the third and last time at the age of 37. Little is recorded of his doings in the Melbourne press, but it is noted that he was the first man to be booed off a football field, in Ballarat after Geelong travelled by train to play the miners on a day of strong wind and rain. After his team failed to goal in the first half with the gale behind them, Tommy instructed them to kick the ball out of play at every opportunity in the second, thereby denying the home side any chance to score. 'The bell to signal the end of the game was met by a cacophony of hissing and cat-calls and unseemly cries directed against the captain of the Geelong team, Mr T.W. Wills!' Tommy strides unrepentant from the field, the sea of angry faces parting before him. A section of the crowd has been drinking. One hour later, their faces are still pressed against the dressing-room's wire windows, the police continue to be anxious about the possibility of a riot, and Tommy is sitting in a corner, grinning. 'The demons are outside,' he tells his players.

'The general belief in the [Melbourne] club was that Wills was never the same after the massacre in which his father and 17 others perished on the Nogoa River in Queensland.' (William Tennant, 'Fine Leg' of the *Australasian*)

Alfred Bonicelli, 'Spectator' of the *Melbourne Illustrated News*

> After the tour of England, Mullagh, the star Aboriginal batsman, was engaged for a period by the Melbourne Cricket Club as a professional. Mullagh performed creditably, even representing the Colony, but, like all blacks, he pined for the place of his birth. Eventually, he fell sick with inflamation of the lungs and the threat to life was such it was decided to release him from his contract and send him home. I remember mentioning this to Tom Wills, asking what he thought would become of Mullagh. T.W.W. was sitting on the benches outside the members' pavilion reading a newspaper, pads on, waiting to bat. He paused in his reading for only a moment, and said, 'He'll die.' A number of fellows who heard the exchange laughed and it became a story told about him, one he dismissed with a shrug.

The public falling-out between Wills and Tennant, or, put another way, Tommy's fall from public grace. This is it in full, or very near to, beginning with Tennant's report in the *Australasian* of 11 January 1873 of the Grand Inter-colonial Match between Victoria and New South Wales at the Melbourne Cricket Ground. T. W. Wills, the captain of the Victorian XI, the drunk who never drank on match day, has turned up pissed.

> Victoria played virtually only ten men, as Wills was of no use what-ever. I think that no-man should be elected captain in a cricket match about whose ability to first' captain himself' there is any doubt. It brings the game into disrepute; but it has so long been rank heresy to say a word against Wills that it is hazardous to do so now, at the risk of

having all the malignant scribblers down on me in a pack. At last he got no-balled, and by a Sydney umpire, who, to his credit, showed his impartiality by also no-balling Dave Gregory. Now that Wills has retired for good I hope that throwing will be put down effectually. Mr Curtis has set a good example, which all umpires here must follow, whether the mob likes it or not. Members of clubs can soon prevent the mob from taking the law into their own hands on cricket grounds, as there has been a disposition to do, I am sorry to notice, of late. The larrikin element must be kept under, otherwise there is an end of all law and order on cricket grounds.

T.W.W. in reply

Dear Sir,

I shall be exceedingly obliged if you will allow me space to make a few comments on an article, written by one 'Fine Leg' in the columns of your Collins Street contemporary. I may here remark that the same writer has for the past three years been in the habit of writing me down whenever he thought it would do me an injury, allowing me no opportunity of replying in the columns over which he presides; but, really, every cricketer knows the man and how very contemptible he is. Did he not try to cast cold water on the late match, and allude to the Sydney players as professionals (as if it were a dishonest profession?). I can remember the time when 'Fine Leg' would have been hard up indeed if it had not been for the poor contemptible lot of the professional cricketer. I once had the pleasure of playing under 'Fine Leg' as captain in an Inter-colonial match and a bigger old woman never held the position, yet forsooth he talks about the captainship of the late match, etc. Allow me to inform him that it was not bad generalship that lost the match, but bad batting, worse fielding and miserable bowling. What could anyone do in such a state of things? However, just to annoy him, I will strive next year to occupy the same position and try to win, although he seems to think different. Furthermore, I will captain a team with anyone in the world, bar none. The greatest mistake I made in the recent match was in not going in earlier each innings, for I was in better batting form than fully one half the team. In the future I shall never again take the slightest notice of 'Fine Leg's' bilious contributions, but treat them with the contempt they deserve.

I am, etc.

'Fine Leg' bites back

Unlike most men who excel in anything, Mr Wills is very vain of himself and his abilities. He thinks Victoria has won all her matches through him alone, and that everyone else is 'an old woman' - 'Fine Leg' especially. He forgets Victoria has won under captains other than him. 'Fine Leg' may be an old woman as a captain, but in the only match you served under him, Mr Wills, there was certainly another old woman in the team, who, fresh from England and Rugby, got a 'duck's egg' and a 'single' in the two innings. I wonder if you remember that old woman, Mr Thomas Wentworth Wills? There was 'an old woman' who played some years ago for the South Melbourne club against the MCC when the latter had the great Wills and Conway bowling for them. And 'the old woman' broke both those bowlers' hearts, until somebody threw a ball that bumped and hit the 'old woman' on the elbow, giving him an Injury from which he suffers to this day. Do you remember that 'old woman' who scored nearly 90 runs against Wills and Conway, and was 'not out (hurt)', in the first innings, and 'run out' in the second? That Old Woman could play Wills now on a good wicket for a month of Sundays if he did not throw. Many matches have been won not through your captaincy, Mr Wills, but in spite of it, for if ever there was a selfish captain who considered 'self' first and 'the match' afterwards that captain was Tommy Wills. You have been a great cricketer, no doubt; a middling bat, and a very ugly one; but as a bowler you would have been played out long ago had the umpires 'no-balled' you as you should have been, and will be now if you try your dodges on again. But it is not likely you will ever have a chance of captaining Victoria again. I will give you a little parting advice, Mr Wills. You are played out now, the cricketing machine is rusty and useless, all respect for it is gone. You will never be the captain of a Victorian Eleven again, that you may be sure of. You are really an old woman now, like 'Fine Leg'. Settle down quietly at Geelong, dear Geelong. Eschew colonial beer, and take the pledge, and in time your failings may be forgotten and only your talents as a cricketer remembered. Farewell, Tommy Wills.

The Editor of the *Australasian*

Mr T.W. Wills is aggrieved by some expressions used by 'Fine Leg' in a recent issue of this journal. The two cricketing lights have been roundly abusing each other in print and the dispute has

Now reached a point at which Mr Wills considers himself injuriously treated. There is no doubt that 'Fine Leg' was a rough antagonist. The letter that Mr Wills complains of contained some expressions of an intemperate character that would have been better omitted. There were personal allusions in it that ought not have been employed towards an old cricketer like Mr Wills, and we are sorry that we admitted them into our columns. But Mr Wills must remember that he gave very gross provocation. The letter to which these strictures was a reply was as offensive an attack as could be penned, and contained some insinuations the legal aspects of which may possibly form the subject of more exact discrimination in an authoritative quarter.

'Once he couldn't play cricket any more, no-one wanted to know him.' (Sally Wills [Barber], T.W.'s de facto for the last three years, 4 May 1880.)

From *Cricketing Reminiscences and Personal Recollections* W.G. Grace 1899

Of course cricket like this cannot be taken seriously, and the match in Kadina (March 1874) is scarcely worth recording at all. One or two incidents which happened made it memorable. Mr. T.W. Wills, the old Rugbeian, had been coaching the Kadina team for over a month in view of the match, and as he had been instructing them in the game the Kadina people thought a good deal of his prowess, and expected him to do valiantly against us. He made a pair of spectacles - clean bowled in each innings - and after that the Kadina people were interested in him no more. Another reminiscence of the match may be interesting. When Mr. Bush went in to bat he missed the first ball, and was clean bowled. As he was the last man in, the Kadina men began to move towards the tent, but Bush, in the coolest possible manner, picked up the stump, put it in the ground, and turning to the umpire, said, 'That was only my trial ball. I always insist on having a trial'; whereupon the umpire, no doubt thinking that Bush knew more about cricket than he did, said, 'Certainly, sir,' and gave him in.

Age of the Great W.G. in March 1874? Twenty-six. Tom Wills? Thirty-nine. By then, Tommy was gone. I've seen it in other old champions. Ball past them before they can get the bat to it. None of the old tricks help, not shuffling across the stumps, nor fixing the eyes till they hurt. Running in to bowl is harder too. The young T.W.W. was like a dancer moving with lethal intent, now his joints creak and ache. Actions once as free as circles now have to be forced to a conclusion. In the first innings, he let the locals do the bowling. In the second, he had no choice. Wills, T.W. (capt.): 72

balls, 28 runs, 6 wickets - including Grace, caught Bails bowled Wills 54. W.G. didn't tell his readers that. A terrible wicket by all reports, pebbly and loose, but still no reason to believe the Great Man gave his wicket away. W.G. never gave his wicket away: that's the legend, isn't it? Nor did W.G. see fit to tell his readers that he cheated the promoters, signing a contract to play only the one match in South Australia, against the York Peninsula, then competing for regional prestige with the city of Adelaide on the basis of the wealth of its copper mines. As soon as the match ended, the Englishmen boarded an overnight coach and the following morning, tired and cramped after a 14-hour journey, took the field against the South Australian Cricket Association on their Adelaide ground for 110 pounds in cash, plus half the gate proceeds. 'Words fail toexpress the indignation felt by everyone here at the base and scoundrelly treatment the Peninsula has received from the gentlemen (?) players known as the All-England Eleven.' (The *Wallaroo Times*)

But, no doubt, in one respect, Dr Grace was right. No doubt, in the end, the crowd did turn away from Tommy Wills. In the end, they always do, leaving individuals who have known intimations of immortality in their youth to suffer the daily pangs of ordinariness. In fact, Tommy and W.G. met more than once. Grace wrote that there wasn't a dusty town on the whole continent that T.W. Wills wasn't prepared to represent.

T.W.W. to the secretary of the MCC, October 1877. The look of the words upon the page? Large and ordered, like a once proud fleet which has prepared itself to be boarded:

W.H. Handfield Esq.
Acting Hon Sec Melbourne Cricket Club
Dear Sir,
Seeing by Advertisement that applications are to be sent in to you for the office of Secretary to the MCC I herewith apply for same. I am well up in the duties attached to the office and do not fear work and I trust that the Committee will give my application a favourable consideration owing to my many years' devotion to Colonial Cricket. I am, Dear Sir,
Yours Truly,
Thomas W. Wills

Not a chance. Mr Handfield shakes his head and puts the letter to one side. Poor old Tom.

Alfred Bonicelli

Tom Wills I last encountered standing alone in the Richmond Paddock beside an old white gum tree watching a game of football being played on the slope below. I approached him and hailed him in a familiar manner, but having acknowledged my arrival with a nod (but not, I noted, my name), his attention returned to the game. The Geelong club was playing Melbourne and having gone down the slope in the first period of play and failed to score any goals; the visitors were obliged to defend for the whole of the second half. This they did stoutly, until in the final minute a young Geelong defender mistakenly passed the ball to a Melbourne man who slipped through his grip and goaled. The bell clanged ending the match and the crowd's cry, signalling both delight and disappointment, rang up the slope. The goal scorer was mobbed by supporters and his fellow players, while the young Geelong man was left sitting on the ground on his own, head between his knees. That was when my companion spoke. 'Someone should go to him,' he said, pointing. As always, there was something in what he said but before I could respond he turned on his heel and strode off. My last view of the Grace of Colonial Cricket, dear reader, was of a figure striding off in the direction of the city with the uncertain tread of the habitually intoxicated man. *Quam Cito Transit Gloria Mundi!*

Sally Wills, Torn Wills's de facto wife and his junior by 15 years, said he would shake her awake in the night and tell her to dress for church, that they were going to pray for forgiveness, or he would order her to look out the window. 'They don't make any noise,' he would say. 'You know that, don't you?' He could babble on like this for hours. In the morning she'd find him slumped in a chair by the fireplace, head to one side, mouth open, looking curiously like a child. On waking, he would immediately don the armour of his formal self, but each day he was a little more pale, a little more spent. If she tried to discuss the events of the night, he would dismiss the subject. The most he said was that he sometimes slept badly. Always had, even as a child. Strange dreams about animals that returned to him in Queensland. Just once he said, 'This is a bloody fearful land.'

Visitors rarely visited their small cottage in Heidelberg because he was argumentative in drink. Colden came now and then in his dark suits and high white collars. With his grey hair and quiet good looks, he reminded her of a doctor. He would sit with Tommy, sharing his silences, nodding in agreement at his words. They never argued, they never had. Tom Wills was the person who would play with anyone. The only catch was that you had to play by his rules and Colden always had. Why not? When it came to sport, Tommy knew best. His enemies had never defeated him on the field of play. Oh no, to bring him down they had resorted to the hidden levers that control committees and the press. Not that he bore them any deep ill will. Why should he? They were so much less than himself-that had always been his point. But now the playing field was no longer there for him. 'So go to work Tom & do your duty & remember your Father's words, "Work like a man".' But there was no work for Tommy Wills. Each day, he read the newspaper a little more quickly, flinging it aside with the words, 'Nothing. Nothing for someone like me.'

Occasionally, in the early hours of the afternoon, she would find him standing in his vegetable patch beneath a benign blue sky, pipe in hand, looking across the valley to the calm blue line of the Dandenongs. He was still as straight as a tree, and his remaining curls were wirier than ever. At such moments, he could briefly admit her presence. She would put an arm around his waist and for a minute or two they would hold one another like pieces of driftwood on an increasingly dangerous sea. Soon enough, they would be parted. Around gloaming, as each day ended and the broad plain between the cottage and the Dandenongs became subsumed by halflight, she would find him standing at the cottage door, an anxious look on his face, and before long he would stride past her, eyes averted, open the cupboard door beneath the dresser and take out a bottle. Once he started drinking he didn't stop, wrapping himself in the spirit's brutal embrace until it rendered him unconscious. She drank with him. That way, at least, they shared their loneliness. Then, after two or three hours' numb slumber, he would wake *like he was on fire.*

The last letters. Written on the same day -12 March 1880- to Cedric and Horace Wills, Cullin-la-ringo station, Queensland. One thanks Horace for the ten pounds he has sent, the other asks Cedric for that amount. 'I'm out of the world here & the only news I pick up is from the *Age* & that's full of nothing but electioneering businefs.' Businefs-an 18th-century spelling. In a sense, Tom Wills is an 18th-century character, a man of fixed beliefs, and, by now the 20th century is kicking in the womb. A major debate about the existence of God initiated by an employee of the Public Library, Mr Marcus Clarke, through an essay titled 'Civilization Without Delusion' is spilling over into the pages of the *Age* and the *Argus*. That's so much nonsense to Tommy. Of course, the Father exists. Marcus Clarke's other great contribution to colonial life has been his novel, *For the Term of His Natural Life,* a Gothic melodrama which has fixed Tasmania in the Victorian imagination as a place of bestial horror, a dystopic Hell that shadows the high public aspirations of the good people of Victoria. 'Ten pounds from each would clear up my debts & let me get a new start.' Where to this time? Tasmania. Tommy says Tasmania has openings for people like him. Sure it does. Old Buck finished his days down there as the turnkey at the women's prison. Wept when he heard of the first massacre of blacks by whites in Port Phillip. Why wouldn't he? He had Aboriginal children. Died drunk when he was run over by a cart in Arthur's Circus, Battery Point.

'The colony is in a slump.' In fact, it is at the beginning of a boom, one funded by foreign capital that will establish Melbourne, now connected by telegraph to the outside world, as a metropolis of international renown. Over the next decade, the city will acquire its neo-classical facades, its manufacturing base will quadruple and its population will double, largely at the expense of country Victoria. Melbourne will be compared to Chicago and San Francisco as one of the wonders of the modem world. To enhance the image of Marvellous Melbourne, as it is called by an anxious to please English journalist, the slums and brothels at the end of Bourke and Little Lonsdale Streets will be pushed north into the suburb of Fitzroy. The area of bush between the MCG and the city will be converted into parklands and the Melbourne Cricket Club's original weatherboard pavilion will be sold 'as it stands' for 56 pounds. Work has begun on St Paul's Church of England Cathedral, opposite Flinders Street station, and there is excitement about the forthcoming Grand Exhibition to be held in the new Exhibition Building in Carlton Gardens. It will have 32,000 exhibits from around the world and a display of the latest inventions from America-among them, the lawnmower, the typewriter and the hydraulic lift. 'The Prince and Princess of Wales are expected for the opening of the Great Exhibition. That will draw a crowd - trains now run to all parts of the colony.' The most talked-about painting in the Exhibition Gallery, one which will give . Melbourne the thrill of scandal, is of a nude girl by the French artist Lefebevre called *Chloe.*

An English visitor to Melbourne declares the *Argus* to be the best newspaper in the world outside London, but for the past two years the biggest news story in the land has been strictly local, centering on the continued inability of the Victorian Police, led by an incompetent from the Melbourne Club called Captain Standish, to apprehend a gang of young bushrangers operating in the colony's mountainous north-east. There is persistent talk among the outlaw's mostly Irish Catholic followers of establishing an independent republic in north-eastern Victoria, and the gang's tactic in attempting to derail a train of troopers foreshadows those employed fifteen years later in South Africa by Boer farmers. The plan is foiled; Ned Kelly is wounded twice in 'the first volley' but escapes. The following morning, wearing a suit of armour, he steps out of the mist firing a pistol and advances on the small army of troopers and black trackers surrounding his 19-year-old brother and another gang member in the Glenrowan Hotel. One reporter at the scene likens the impact of his appearance to Hamlet seeing his father's ghost. Eventually shot in his unprotected knees, Ned topples and is finally captured. It is 20 years since there has been a similar challenge to the authorities in New South Wales, 50 years in Tasmania. Changes in newspaper technology have also made Ned the first *illustrated* bushranger and a hero to the colony's larrikin class. Brought to trial in the Supreme Court of Victoria before Sir Redmond Barry, Ned says his mind is easy before God. Sir Redmond says it is blasphemous for him to say so. Ned tells Sir Redmond he will meet him in that place to which he is going and, 13 days after he drops, pinioned and bound, through the metal scaffold in the Old Melbourne Gaol, Sir Redmond dies from blood poisoning caused by a boil on the back of his neck.

This is the great popular drama of the day. Tommy hears none of it. 'I thought you both lived at the old head station, but it seems that you live some distance apart, I never hear any news.' Horace is under the impression that Tommy receives five pounds a week, which is a great mistake. He receives three pounds per week from the trustees, but they retain one pound to pay-off some old debts in Geelong. If he gets 10 pounds from Cedric he will clear off to Tasmania, not trouble anyone again and repay as soon as he can. Tasmania is the place for Tommy. 'Write to me some time, old man. Heidelberg is so quiet I think the government is about to fall.'

Alfred Bonicelli wrote that T.W. Wills died of softening of the brain.

William Tennant said privately that he had seen it before in other old cricketers who played the game in that way. 'When there are no more poor batsmen to stand at the other end of the pitch as the objects of their loathing and scorn, they have to turn and face themselves.' Publicly he said that if Tom Wills had an enemy, that enemy was himself alone.

J.B. Ellis, 'Fair Play' of the *Argus*, said Wills was taciturn by nature but a general favourite. 'If he ever spoke a serious word on a subject other than cricket, I never heard it'.

Horace Wills said his brother was a wild, reckless individual but one of the best people he had ever met. He said the reason he drank too much was because people were always buying him drinks and it wasn't in his nature to disappoint.

Sally Wills said he was two people.

The Age noted his death only briefly, but placed it above an account of the execution of an Indian named Swift Runner in Saskatchewan, Canada. A priest seeking to offer consolation on the scaffold to the Indian was motioned away by the condemned man. The white man's whisky spirit had ruined him, he said, so he had no reason to believe in the white man's God. Instead, he asked his people gathered at the foot of the gallows to perform a death dance. When the rope broke on the first drop, the Indian offered to kill himself with a tomahawk.

And his mother, Elizabeth Wills, cried out, 'Thomas - I never had a son called Thomas!'. That's when Tommy began to disappear. He stabbed himself in the heart.

Tom Wills by William Handcock.

7
Thereafter

A green sign above the motorway says Heidelberg. Possibly the most famous school in the history of Australian art was based here at the end of the nineteenth century. Streeton, Roberts, McCubbin, Condor all travelled the few miles from Melbourne to Heidelberg to capture the paper-dry light of the Australian summer. They painted the taciturn bush as it follows the winding line of the river and the lightly wooded plains stretching to the blue lumps of the Dandenongs. A decade earlier the former cricketer T.W. Wills had resided in the area, bored out of his wits. Much like his old man had been when he was sequestered down at Geelong. In the hundred years since artists camped in the area, Heidelberg's grass plains became market gardens and small farms and these, in turn, became small towns, until now Heidelberg is a part of Melbourne like all the other outer suburbs, carpeted with newsagents, hot-bread bakeries, houses, service stations, car yards and shopping-centres, and divided by motorways.

The Old Heidelberg Cemetery, as it is called, is opposite a multi-storeyed hospital for motor accident victims with large glass windows that blankly reflect the sky. Built in the Georgian style, on the eastern aspect of a hill, the cemetery's high red brick walls are lined with cypress trees. When T.W. Wills was buried here, it was mostly rude green earth. Subsequently, the cemetery was filled to overflowing. Graves lie cracked and open, lids falling off to one side; marble crosses tilt out of the earth, as if the dead have staged an uprising and moved to other places. At first the local authority told me they had no record of any T.W. Wills being buried on the site but I insisted. Two weeks later, I received a plan of the cemetery with the plot marked in orange text a and a computer printout of the information recorded at the time the body was interred:

DECEASED'S NAME: WILLS T.W. AGE: 44 YEARS.
BORN: 01/01/1836.

Wrong day; wrong month, wrong year. January 1 is the birth date given where the actual date is unknown or not given - that is, for vagrants and Aborigines.

DIED: 04/05/1880.

Wrong again. He died on the 2nd (Sunday) and was buried on the 4th

(Tuesday). The inquest was on the Monday. Deceased's de facto said he had been drinking heavily for years and that his final bout had lasted several days. A neighbour, Mr Darmoody, testified he had observed the deceased, dressed in church clothes, feeding his hens on Sunday morning. He heard him talking, saying brightly to each of the hens, 'Eat up. This is the last meal you'll be getting from Old Tom.' In the early hours of Saturday morning, Mr Darmoody's wife had beheld the deceased on the verandah of his cottage waving his arms and arguing with a phantom, but Mr Darmoody now observed Wills to be in better spirits than he had been for months. (He otherwise described him as 'a moody man who seldom spoke'.) At the request of Sally Wills, Darmoody entered the house around noon on Sunday and assisted in removing any dangerous object he spied, as the deceased was talking openly of killing himself. His life, he told Darmoody, was of no use. After Darmoody had gone, Wills first tried to kill himself by placing a hand over his nose and holding his breath. Having failed to despatch himself in that manner, he strode into the kitchen, located a knife in a drawer and, holding off his de facto wife with his left arm, inflicted three wounds in his chest, the third of which touched his heart. After inflicting the fatal wound, he sank to the floor. He did not speak again.

TIME OF BURIAL: 8:00 A.M.

Heidelberg is 10 miles, or two hours by carriage from Melbourne, How many people were going to be able to make a funeral at eight o'clock in the morning? In the event, only four did-Egbert Wills, Colden Harrison, Emily Harrison and a representative of the Melbourne Cricket Club. Sally Wills's whereabouts on the day are unknown, but a letter from Egbert Wills to his brothers in Queensland says the family is prepared to pay £100 a year to 'keep her away'.

TYPE OF GRAVE: EARTH.

Tommy was buried like a piece of meat

Thereafter it's Colden's story, mostly. In 1908, the Jubilee of Australian Football was held in Melbourne. All six states of the newly formed Commonwealth of Australia attend, plus New Zealand, the New Zealand team travelling for two weeks, by ship and train, to participate. Arriving at Spencer Street railway station, they were met by the organising committee and driven to a match being played on the East Melbourne ground between Essendon and Melbourne. At halftime, the competing teams lined up to give the visitors three cheers. The New Zealanders responded in kind, throwing their hats into the damp winter air. *Hip hip! Hurrah!*

The evening before the final round of matches, a smoke night is held at the Melbourne Town Hall in Swanston Street. Distinguished guests include the Prime Minister, Mr Alfred Deakin, a number of members of the newly elected federal legislature, the Chief Commissioner of the Victoria Police, and the Vice-president of the Executive Council. However, the evening's guest of honour is the recently retired Registrar of Titles for Victoria, Mr H.C.A. Harrison, now aged 73. Five hundred guests, all male, fill the body of the hall so that the evening begins with a restless commotion of sound. This abates when the hall is darkened for a biograph of a recent match between the Bendigo and Eaglehawk teams, and when the hall is again lightened all rise for the loyal toast. *To the King!* The audience noisily resume their seats, and the Prime Minister alone remains standing, having been asked by the organisers to propose the toast to the Australasian Game of Football.

Alfred Deakin is elegant and bearded like the Russian Tsar. He calls himself an Australian Briton and, at the age of 52, is proud that his baritone voice reveals no trace of a provincial accent. Born in Collingwood of English parents who arrived in Victoria during the Gold Rush, he is regarded as an inspirational orator, although papers discovered after his death will reveal that his eloquence masked a deep inner melancholy. A man of genuine intellectual breadth, he reads German and Greek and has delved deeply into spiritualism. A barrister who has dabbled in journalism, principally for the *Age,* he has, in good part, arrived at his political pre-eminence through his relationship with David Syme, the proprietor of that newspaper. Syme persuaded Deakin of the need for government protection of Victorian manufacturing industry; in return, Deakin, a member of the Australian Natives' Association, persuaded Syme of the case for federation. Victoria has been the driving force behind forging the newly created Commonwealth of Australia and, pending the construction of a national capital, the Commonwealth Parliament, as well as the major government departments, are situated in Melbourne.

'My days as a footballer are long past,' begins Deakin, 'but I have a recollection that the game I played had rules rather more liberal than those experienced by footballers today.' *[Laughter]* In fact, he was a clumsy footballer. 'Then it was a Victorian game, and it is a very great gain to now find it an Australasian game. *[Applause]* This country, with its sunny skies and green fields, its ample time for leisure, will ensure that we remain what we have always been-a sporting people.' *[Cheers]* Deakin believes Australia must be capable of defending itself; to this end, he has recently introduced a bill into the federal parliament providing for compulsory military service. 'There was a time when Great Britain's indulgence in sport was looked upon as insular, but in the last thirty to forty years a remarkable change has become apparent over the whole of Europe. In every nation, there has been a rebirth of sport with the recognition of the part it plays in the national life, not merely in physical training, but the discipline of sport, its effect upon character and courage.' War is looming in Europe. Sport is always being pushed in one political direction or another. 'In the last resort, a nation's name and indeed its very existence is staked upon its young men and should the call to arms be sounded in this land the first, not the last, to acknowledge it will be those who have played, and played well, the Australian game of football.' [*Prolonged cheering*]

In response, Mr C.M. Hickey, President of the Australasian Football Council, thanks the Prime Minister for 'his words. He is followed by Mr J.J. Jones of the West Australian league. A plump young man with ruddy cheeks and curly black hair who speaks with a ringing cadence, Jones is a rising figure in West Australian social and political circles. Gesturing towards the slight, immaculately dressed figure three places away from him at the head table, Jones begins by saying, 'No man in the sporting world of Australia has such a unique claim to our regard and respect as this evening's guest of honour.' He recounts that Colden Harrison's time of 50.25 seconds for the quarter-mile, recorded in 1861, was for many years regarded as a world record. He was five times Champion of the Colony at Football and, at the age of 63, this in defatigable athlete had taken it upon himself to cycle from Melbourne to Sydney. 'But the man who excels at sport is not half so rare as our guest of honour. For many years, Mr Harrison was one of Victoria's most senior public servants, yet, despite the rigours and demands of his employment, he continued to serve tirelessly on committees promoting manly sport in general and the Australasian game in particular. It is his special distinction, and ours, that he is as much an example as a citizen as he was as a sportsman. Gentlemen, I give you the Father of Australian Football.'

His words are met with prolonged cheering, waves of noise that rise up from the body of the hall, accumulating in strength. Colden Harrison stands alone, a slim, silver-haired man with the faint flicker of a smile on his face. Eventually, all stand to applaud him. When finally the audience takes their seats, his speech is modest and mildly amusing. He recalls the old days, playing on 'the gravel pit' outside the MCG, and some of the game's early characters. He tells, as he always does, how as a youth of 16 he determined not to drink beer or spirits until he was fully grown, nor to partake of tobacco, and that, throughout his long life, he has always valued open-air exercise. 'Nowadays, that means working in my garden.' Polite laughter, followed by extended applause which becomes a second ovation. The evening ends with the New Zealand and Queensland teams startling the audience with renditions of their native war cries. Victoria is among the states with no memory of such things.

'Blazing Trails Sporting and Pastoral' - third and final start (written about 10 years later):

> The first Aboriginal team of Australian cricketers that toured Australia and defeated the Army and Navy combined cricket club on the Sydney Cricket Ground in the presence of the Duke of Edinburgh, visited England in season 1868 under the management of Charles Lawrence. Naturally, it was the dominating influence of Tom Wills who coached the team in Australia that made it possible for the adventure to succeed for the bulk of the players, including the famous dusky batsman Johnny Mullagh, were drawn from the Western District in the vicinity of Lake Wallace. What a wonderful demonstration to the world was this! Here we have the example of two men, T.W. Wills, a native born Australian, and Charles Lawrence, an Englishman, gathering together a band of native aboriginal cricketers, educating and leading them under the gentle and humanising laws of cricket and playing the game in the company of and against the finest players of the game in the world! What an object lesson to humanitarians of all creeds and classes, and what an incentive such an example should have been to all Australian governments as to their attitude and treatment of Australia's rapidly vanishing race. Alas, it is now all but forgotten.

The pavilion from which Colden Harrison and Sir Arthur Conan Doyle watched the 1920 grand final between Richmond and South Melbourne at the Melbourne Cricket Ground was not the pavilion that is there now -a plain low-slung thing built in the 1920s- but a double-storeyed Victorian structure with lace verandahs and a sloping slate roof. All eyes had been upon the short sturdy figure in the tweed suit as he entered the Long Room, but he was accustomed to that. A large white moustache flowed to both sides of his pink face and his manner was brusque and certain, although a perceptive observer might have noted that his eyes always seemed to be a thought ahead of his words. Sir Arthur was in Melbourne on a mission. Attending a seance in Wales after losing his son in World War I, a grief-stricken Sir Arthur had heard his son's voice and been converted to spiritualism: he was in Australia propagating the belief that it is possible to communicate with the dead. Letter writers to the *Argus* called him a shaman and a crank, a representative of evil, but he was used to that. His speaking tours in Britain inevitably attracted similar responses. 'Why is it,' he asked the packed houses who came to hear him speak, 'that my enemies invariably fall into two camps-fundamentalists and "free" thinkers?' And it was not as if the abuse kept the crowds away. After all, this was the man who had imagined into being one of the best-known minds of the preceding century, that of Mr Sherlock Holmes.

The pre-match luncheon in the Melbourne Cricket Clubs committee room included a number of speeches, in the course of which Sir Arthur received a full bouquet of compliments. He was said to have been a keen sportsman in his youth, having played both rugby and soccer, and, as his writings attested, he was an enthusiast for boxing, so it was hoped he would be favourably impressed by the Australian game. Sir Arthur was seated at the head table beside the man who had been on the committee of the Melbourne Cricket Club for more than 50 years and vice-president for nearly 30, Colden Harrison. When the game began, Harrison led his guest out onto the balcony where travelling rugs were placed over their knees and drinks served to them by a waiter with oiled hair and commendable reserve.

Sir Arthur was favourably impressed by the game.

There was no offside, and you got a free kick if you caught the ball. Otherwise you ran, as in rugby, though there was a law about bouncing the ball as you ran, which he felt could be cut out without harming the game. He later wrote, 'This bouncing rule was put in by Mr Harrison who drew up the original rules, for the chivalrous reason that he was himself the fastest runner in the Colony, and he did not wish to give himself any advantage.'

Not so fast, Sir Arthur. Negotiations on the subject of running with the ball began only after the Royal Park club unearthed a player as quick as Colden Harrison-some said quicker. It was not in Colden's nature to surrender an advantage. In later years, when his legs began to slow, he even acquired a reputation for occasional meanness in his play.

In all, Colden Harrison was Vice-president of the Melbourne Cricket Club for 36 years. In his autobiography *The Story of an Athlete* he said he never sought the presidency of the club, and one suspects this is true. Colden Harrison never forgot where he came from. The knowledge terrified him. His autobiography begins with the words, 'I am as old as Melbourne.' Well, yes, as old as Melbourne, but not as old as the settlement, with its two flawed founders, Batman and Fawkner. Colden Harrison was born the year Captain Lonsdale sailed down from Sydney to impose law and order on the residents of Bearbrass, also known as Phillipi on the Yarra. In his autobiography, Colden Harrison makes no mention of his convict grandfather, George Howe (a.k.a. George Happy or Happy George), nor is there any reference to the raft of convict relatives he acquired through his double connection with the Wills family. His father's role as one of the principal agitators on the Victorian goldfields is also overlooked, as is the fact that in later life his father, the self-styled Captain Harrison, publicly decried Queen Victoria's children as a burden on colonial tax-payers and achieved considerable notoriety by burning an effigy of the Governor at Williamstown railway station.

His happiest days, he wrote, were those he had spent on the balcony of the MCC pavilion, watching world class sport, chatting and nodding to acquaintances. 'One of his daughters is the wife of Mr B.H. Friend, the ex-chief of the Federal Hansard staff.' His book is full of asides like that, references to people of standing in Melbourne society and their connections. It was noted that Colden went to games alone and the few references to his wife in *The Story of an Athlete* are distant and formal. On his return to England, Sir Arthur Conan Doyle wrote, 'There is a sort of Australian who is more English than the English. We have been imperceptibly Americanised, while our bretheren over the sea have kept to the old type. The Australian is less ready to show emotion, cooler in his bearing, more restrained in applause, the more devoted to personal liberty, keener on sport, and quieter in expression.' A black-and-white photograph of H.C.A. Harrison in his 90th year shows him standing, slim and erect, hands by his side, in front of a flagpole in the garden of his ample home in the affluent suburb of Kew. The flag beneath which he stands is the Union Jack.

And what of his cousin Tom Wills, who stabbed himself in the heart and was not spoken about thereafter in polite company, what does Colden Harrison say about him? He says that when Tommy returned to the colony from England in 1856, he was the *beau ideal* of an athlete. That's strong language for Colden. He recalls that while captaining the Victorian XI against New South Wales, his cousin sustained a compound fracture of the middle finger of his right hand, notwithstanding which he came out and won the match! He also says that when Tom Wills died the newspapers stressed his kindly nature as much as his sporting skills, but he makes no mention of the manner of his death. Elsewhere in his memoirs, however, he does give a brief account of the Cullin-la-ringo massacre, observing that Horatio Wills's death occurred in the same year as the two Victorian explorers Burke and Wills perished in their heroic attempt to cross the continent from north to south. According to H.C.A. Harrison, the Cullin-la-ringo massacre was caused by 'the cupidity of the natives', their natural greed having been excited by the many open boxes lying around the camp. Wrong. At least, it's not what his cousin thought.

Cedric Wills, the Rockhampton *Daily Record*, 8 November 1912

In order that a correct version of what is known as the murder of the Wills family over fifty years ago in the Springsure district may be given to the public, Mr Cedric Wills, of Minerva Creek station, has by request supplied the following details:

'The tragedy took place on the 16th of October, 1861. Before the arrival of the Willses on Garden Creek, where the murder was committed, the blacks were collecting on the Nogoa River, at the foot of Separation Creek, with the object of attacking Mr Jesse Gregson, the first owner who stocked Rainworth and who with a detachment of native police had shot some blacks for the supposed stealing of sheep prior to the arrival of our party. My oldest brother Tom, who came out with the party and happened to be away with two teams and the drivers at the time of the murder, told me, "If the truth ever be known, you will find that it was through Gregson shooting the blacks; that was the cause of the murder,"

'Of course, it was years before the blacks were allowed in again, and even then none would own up to any knowledge of the murder, till one day my brother Horace and I had a boy out helping to muster sheep, and we were trying to find out from him the cause, when all at once he said, "What for white fellow shoot um blackfellow first time?" Directly he said this, I knew what he meant, but pretended to know nothing about it and got him to tell me all.

'It seems that Gregson had not counted his sheep for a week or so, and all this time the blacks had seen a small mob of lost sheep, and this boy said, "Carra moochalodienn." (There were no shepherd's foot-tracks with the sheep.) He also said, "Blackfellow think white fellow throw 'em away." After several days of seeing them wandering about, one morning the blacks made a small yard, drove the sheep up to their camp, yarded and killed some, and were cooking the meat on their fires. That same morning, Gregson counted his sheep and found he was short. He went out and found blacks' tracks on the sheep track. Without following them up, he went straight back to camp, and, as there was a detachment of native police that had come the day before, they at once saddled up and Gregson took them to where he had seen the tracks.

'Within a short distance, they came to the camp where the blacks were eating the mutton. The blacks did not think they were doing anything wrong, and never moved or tried to get away. They simply went on cooking the meat as Gregson, the police officer and the troopers rode close up and fired right into the camp. Several blacks were wounded, but the others, though frightened at the noise of the guns, did not run but jumped to their feet. On seeing some of their mates unable to rise and crying out in fright, they knocked Gregson, the officer, and the troopers off their horses with nulla-nullas. Gregson got up and was staggering about and two gins were trying to get him down when the blacks knocked him down again and stunned him properly. In his dazed state, while struggling with the gins, he had pulled out his revolver and fired, but instead of hitting the gins shot the native police officer in the leg.

'The blacks left the party all stunned and carried off their wounded. They could have killed Gregson, the officer and the troopers but did not do so, never thinking that the wounded among their number would die. But after a day some did. Then the others decided to be revenged and attack Gregson and his party. They sent runners all over the country, and were collecting at the foot of Separation Creek, on the Nogoa, which spot was only about six miles from where my father made his camp. It seems Gregson and my father met at times on the run and rode together. Being dressed something alike, and both wearing pith helmets, the blacks took them for brothers, and decided to attack our party, which was nearer to them. Some of the blacks-the younger men and boys-were against the murder, but the elder men threatened to kill them if they divulged their plans, and they were so afraid of the old men that they left the camp.

'The boy that gave me this information showed my brother Horace and me where the young blacks had spent the night previous to the murder. I asked this boy whether, if my father and the bullockdriver had got together and shot one or two blacks, the others would have bolted. He replied, "Carra." (No.) The blacks were in hundreds. Of course I had heard of what Gregson and the native police had done, and being told the same story by this boy convinced me of its truth. It was just as my brother Tom had said. Such acts are mostly the cause of all these murders. It makes my blood boil when I start on this subject-that Gregson, just for the sake of a few sheep, committed the act which was the cause of the murder of my father and all his party, men, women and children.'

Most public figures erode within a few years of their death. Their beliefs read like old labels on empty jars; they are seen as embodying the attitudes of their day and nothing more. Not the case, I would suggest, with Mr T.W. Wills. During his lifetime, pseudo-scientific beliefs about race were part of this country's daily bread-Aboriginal people were the missing link which completed Charles Darwin's chain of evolution, they were less evolved than their Pacific neighbours, they were cannibals who ate their infants; history was the process by which inferior races were eliminated and overrun. Those ideas are still out there, still in circulation, but if Tommy entertained them, he didn't say as much. Basically, I suspect they were superfluous to the world as he saw it. He was, after all, the Grace of Colonial Cricket. *What he lacked he would not need. All that he had he could use.* Alfred Bonicelli, formerly 'Spectator' of the *Melbourne Illustrated News:* 'I once asked Wills if the blacks had been difficult to captain as they have a general reputation for indolence. He said, no, to the contrary. What I understood him to mean was that whereas we Britons will combine for a great cause or if there is a prize to be won, with the blacks it was their natural way.' Tom Wills stands. Not in an obvious way, like a statue outside a building: like a dingo on a plain.

Why, if he had an affinity with the blacks, did he counsel the men in his father's party to carry weapons after they reached Cullin-la-ringo? Because he had been trained for war. He saw it as part of the natural order of things and knew full well the blacks did too.

Besides which, his fear was warranted. Horatio Wills had not only marched blithely into the middle of a land war, he had brought women and children with him. Since his death, Horatio has been flayed for this, including by those who say his only other crime was to trust the blacks and treat them as human. It was Tom's judgment, not his father's, which proved correct, but he still wasn't entrusted with command of the family estate. Tom Wills never grew to manhood in his dead father's eyes. Instead, he stood like a colossus on the diminishing dimensions of 'the field of play' until that, too, went from beneath him like a hangman's trap-door, dropping him into a world of phantoms and hellish disorder which encircled the telescope of his trained mind. At least, in the end, he passed beyond torment and briefly recovered his old certainty. His life was of no use, he said. He had failed, he declared, through his own fault. I'm here to say that's not the case, Tommy.

Each week, I go to the footy. I enter Yarra Park from Punt Road, passing through the native garden and continuing up the rise. I shut out the traffic and think about the place as it once was. Emu about, bush turkey, kangaroo. Fresh water in the river below. Perhaps a solitary eagle somewhere above. For at least 150 years, an old red gum on the other side of the lightly forested slope tilted out of the earth at 45 degrees. Two years ago, after several days of heavy rain, I arrived and found the old tree had toppled under the burden of its eccentric weight. It was lying face down, its exposed roots clutching at the air like a tangle of muddy fists. Young men with chainsaws were slicing it apart and tossing the pieces onto the back of a motorised cart. I picked up a dark red chip and put it in my backpack. That tree was part of the memory of this place. You can see it in a photograph taken from the members' pavilion during the match between H.H. Stephenson's First All-England XI and the Victorian XVIII. Fifteen thousand people in attendance, urchins in the treetops, band in the rotunda. Still in evidence four years later when the Australian Native XI played the Rest of the World XI. The captain of the Native XI, an Old Rugbeian named T.W. Wills, was described, in his youth, as one of the most promising young cricketers in England.

At the top of the rise, surrounded by a rusty iron fence, is the largest of the scarred trees, its upraised arms cropped off at the shoulder, its great heart stripped bare. Sometimes I lean across and rub my hand against the rough black skin of the wound. When something is taken, something, eventually, appears in its place. I have to believe that. This is where I brought young Billy after his mother told me he was on smack. I got him to dance. At first he thought I was joking, but then he saw that I wasn't and went off -wild uninhibited stuff-clapping his hands and slapping his feet. Afterwards we had a talk and I told him about my battle with the grog, about waking with the terrors, facing nothing but an empty black space and the thought that we fall through it one by one. It still comes back if I drink too much, but now I try and get other pictures up on the big screen in my head. A Chinese bloke on the trams told me that if you were in outer space and looked down on the earth you'd say life was one unending force. He made a slow twisting gesture with his hands as he said it and I saw this brilliant blue-green ball slowly spinning through the dark. In this country, for thousands of years, the blackfellahs have celebrated that with song and dance... That's what I told Billy. You can dance in this place. Just acknowledge its spirits as well as your own.

Beneath me, its concrete walls braced with girders and surrounded by light towers, is the MCG. It's housed an army and been blessed by a Pope. It's been the centre stage for an Olympic Games and a venue for rock stars. Sneak in through the groundsmen's entrance one day when it's not in use. Experience the immensity of its silent self; it's like standing on the deck of a giant ghost ship. Then go on match day when thousands of people-men, women and children-are streaming towards it and long queues are radiating from it. As you shoulder through the crowd, the high red-brick wall will periodically shudder with sound. That's what gets my feet moving, hearing a wave of noise rush to climax, retreat, then return again with even greater force as what at first seemed a mere possibility is made fact. Pass through a cranking turnstile into the stadium's huge concrete underbelly. Turning at an oblong patch of light, you climb a set of stairs and are met, first, by the brilliant green of the playing field and, above it, the sheer wall of faces that is the Great Southern Stand. It's in front of the Great Southern Stand that the winning captain on grand final day makes his victory salute. Once, that was done in front of the members' stand on the other side of the ground, but wealth and power have shifted to a new class. They sit behind anonymous glass walls in the corporate boxes. *Some in this colony; whom I would call capitalists, exalt in their riches and have no regard for the First Cause.* Too true, Horatio. The new empire is more discreet than its predecessor. Its leaders don't wear silly costumes in public, but they do make it their business to own all the newspapers and television stations. They also like to own games such as this, that large crowds are in the habit of watching. *Coming events cast their shadow before them.* Yes, yes, Horatio. You fought for free entry into libraries, didn't you, old man? That's now under threat. The poor are getting poorer and more numerous, yet we proceed in the name of Progress. What would Dr Arnold say? I know what I say. *Progress, my arse!* You've probably seen me at the footy. The short, stout, half-bald bloke on the fence with the beer can, shaking his fist at the sky. An angry man, you'd probably think, but one whose rough red face can also register delight and awe.

The reserves match finishes, the playing area is cleared. Clips from famous matches are replayed on large screens at either end of the ground. The fans cheer past triumphs and boo old slights. Cheer squads enter the arena like footmen in a medieval war. Their banners are carefully laid out on the ground, then hauled aloft, people pulling on ropes like sailors in a storm. The great walls of crepe stand taut as spinnakers in a breeze. There is a lull of 10 minutes or so and the teams appear, bursting the banners with the impact of their arrival, then lapping the ground in a group, bodies loose but flexed. Perhaps Carlton is playing, the club of new money. Or perhaps Geelong is in town. Geelong always draw a crowd. They still playas they did in Tommy's day, quick and artful, looking for the space to give expression to their skills. Or maybe it's Essendon. Essendon has a great Aboriginal centreman: the whole game will tilt and sway in anticipation of his thought. Whose game is it, you ask? The blackfellas say it's theirs. The Irish claim they invented it and poor old H.C.A. Harrison went to his grave swearing it was British. If you want my opinion, it's a bastard of a game-swift, bold and beautiful-for a bastard of a people. If it had a white father he wasn't a cautious, calculating fellow like Colden Harrison. He was a reckless young dandy capable of dismissing the suggestion of an English school game with the merest shake of his curly brown head, saying, No, we'll have a game of our own. There were other ways of playing football. He'd seen one as a boy, a game of style and grace played for appreciative audiences. The old men sang the cockatoo Dreaming songs before the young men went out and competed to see who could fly the highest. During the Australian Natives game, Johnny Mullagh recorded the highest jump ever seen in the colony. Imagine seeing him in the air.

The captains toss for choice of ends and report the fall of the coin to their teams with a minimal gesture, a single cocked finger. Great players amble to their positions, their lessers run. Opponents find one another, then with crowd and players alike on edge, a small figure in white bounces the ball. It rebounds into the air, bobbing and floating. Hands rise to meet it. Simultaneously the noise of the crowd's excitement comes out of the earth like a deep-felt explosion. From now until the end, a wild current of hope and fear will charge the stadium and be transmitted around the country on radio. The first rush of play occurs: both sides pursue the ball with vigour and intent. Scoring commences, the match finds a tempo and balance, its first for the afternoon. This will change many times if it is a great game, the balance being altered by individual acts. Then the first of them occurs. A young man does what young men have always dreamed of doing. For an instant, he stands alone in the sky, all others beneath him. The ball arrives, fixing to his outstretched hands; in the same instant, the platform of bodies beneath him collapses and he falls to earth, ball in hand. The crowd's delight is a wild surge of sound. At that moment, all else is forgotten. The flow is within me, a wild dancing light. That's when I make my call, hand cupped to the side of my mouth so that every bastard on earth can hear: *Tom Wills leapt from this land and almost caught the sun.*

Postscript

On September 18 2021, ABC Sport published an article on-line which suggested that Tom Wills may have participated in the mass murder of Aboriginal people during the reprisal attack that followed the Cullin-la-ringo massacre. The effect of this article was described in the following terms by SBS: "Research suggesting Australia's first cricket star and the co-founder of Australian Rules football was involved in the massacre of Aboriginal people has shaken the sporting world".

The ABC report was based on an article that had appeared in 1895 in an American newspaper, the *Chicago Tribune*. Below is my response to the ABC article which was published in *The Age* on September 26 2021. It is followed by an SBS report by Keira Jenkins that was published on October 12 2021 and quotes Darryl Black, an elder of the Gayiri tribe – the people slaughtered in the reprisal raid in which Wills was alleged to have participated. Darryl Black says of the ABC report, ""Thomas Wills we always think he was a great man and was a great friend to the Aboriginal people so I wouldn't want to see his name distorted in any way like that".

Gayiri Country is beautiful, in the way that only some of the most rural parts of Australia can be.

The Age, Martin Flanagan, September 26, 2021

The document which has sparked the latest Tom Wills controversy was published in *The Chicago Tribune* 15 years after Wills's death under the title "Old Days in Australia". My comments on it are interspersed in the text.

"Some time in the 1860s a family of the name of Wills emigrated from England and settled on a nice sheep run in Victoria. Untrue. Both his grandfathers arrived as convicts around 60 years earlier. The family consisted of father, mother, son and three daughters. He had three brothers. I met him in a small town in Victoria..one night after dinner I prevailed upon him to tell the following story which I give in his own words...

This is fictional Tom speaking: *"Well, we had been out here 3 years and had settled down comfortably and were doing well; it was just before Xmas and I had to drive 200 head of cattle and take a lot of wool down to Melbourne and return with the good things for Xmas. I sold everything well, stayed an extra day to see the English fellows play cricket.* Wills was in Queensland when the English cricket team visited Melbourne in 1861 – had he been in Melbourne, he would have played. It is apparent the author doesn't know the massacre and reprisal raids happened in central Queensland, not Victoria.

The following paragraph is critical. *"We had got within about 25 miles from home when something came over me, I cannot explain it; it seemed as if the life had gone out of me, or rather not from me but from someone dear to me. I felt so sick that I got off the pony and told the drivers we would camp for a time. We had a good drink, but that did me no good. Oh God! The agony I suffered during that 25 mile ride, fearful of going too fast, yet wishing to be rid of the awful suspense. At least we got just to the edge of the bush and in two minutes more I knew my fears would be verified, old chap. If ever I offered up an honest prayer I did that moment, and then we came within sight of the house..... I cannot understand it. I had become quite calm, and the sight which met my gaze did not seem to surprise me in the least; in fact, I believe I had a cynical smile on my face, to think how clever I was in divining that something was wrong. And, my God!, there was something wrong, for there, old man, before the very door were the heads of mother, father and three sisters stuck on sticks placed in a row".*

None of this happened. Wills' mother and sisters were in Geelong. This is fiction of a peculiarly American kind written for an American audience. Impaling heads on poles is a recurring nightmare image in American frontier literature. The story about Wills being involved in a reprisal raid which appeared last week on ABC.net did not include this paragraph. It is entirely relevant because, in legal terms, it goes to the credibility of the witness – that is, the anonymous author. But now comes his *coup de grace*!

Fictional Tom speaking again: *"After 8 hours galloping we came up with the band about 3o'clock in the afternoon. What a shout went up as we sighted them. How we galloped down upon them! I cannot tell all that happened, but I know we killed all in sight.* The phrase "but I know we killed all in sight" was used by the ABC to promote the story and has since spread like a virus on social media. *Just as we thought they were all settled I happened to see a dirty, shrinking, greasy brute with my Zingari jacket on slinking off. O , the desecration of it! Fancy my Zingari jacket! O didn't I gallop after him and when I got alongside I buried the whole 6 barrels of my revolver into him. The brute"*.

The anonymous author then abandons the fiction of speaking as Tom and returns to speaking for himself. *"Tommy, poor fellow, took to the drink and became a perfect wreck and if anyone had an excuse for doing so surely he had. It was woe betide any native that came across Tommy Wills, for he was allowed to have a sort of general prescriptive right to rid the country of what he called d-d vermin"*.

This is particularly gross. It's true that Wills said he would shoot any Aboriginal person who returned to the Cullin-la-ringo property in the immediate aftermath of the massacre. But within two years he was accused of having done so, thereby "disgracing" his father's memory. In that period, Wills had spoken to an Aboriginal man, heard the Aboriginal version of the original massacre and believed it, making him, in all probability, the only whitefella in Queensland who did. According to his brother Cedric, he remained of that view for the rest of his life.

So why would the author, identified only as G, fabricate all this? The clue lies earlier in his article when he writes, *"The disappearance of the Aboriginal has also made a change – very much for the better – in the country. It is not for me to judge, but it has ever been a mystery to me why or for what purpose these animals ever had an existence – I say animals advisedly, though in classing them with dogs, horses and animals of that character, I am doing a grievous wrong"*.

The author is the animal. He is a vicious, full-on racist of the sort that would now be termed a domestic terrorist. "Old Days in Australia" is like a bad novel written with malign intent. The author has created a character for Wills who in the act of committing a brutal murder is made to appear gleeful, joyful, psychopathic. It is this image of Wills as an American psycho which looks to have now entered the Australian consciousness.

Nonetheless, when Old Days in Australia was brought to my attention by Gary Fearon, a highly conscientious and fair-minded researcher whose discoveries about Wills extend way beyond this find, I thought, as Fearon did, that it could not be dismissed or ignored. Why can't it be ignored? Because Tom Wills's was a sporting life and, in that sporting life, the I Zingari club played a special part. The I Zingari were a group of aristocrats who played cricket by day and partied by night. Wills played for them after leaving the Rugby school. Five days after returning to Victoria in 1856 as a 21-year-old, Wills appeared at the MCG - where he was, in the words of one journalist, "the most observed of the observed" – wearing his I Zingari colours. This was how he wished to be seen at his coming out.

We also know that during the massacre of the Wills party, their camp was looted and Wills reported his I Zingari "shirts" were stolen. The anonymous American author says the man Wills murdered was wearing an I Zingari "jacket". There is now a furious debate evolving about whether Wills' I Zingari coat made the trip from Victoria to Queensland, whether the terms "shirt" and "jacket" were interchangeable at the time, whether the anonymous American ever actually met Wills etc etc. That debate is right and proper, but it is not where the public focus is.

The ABC, in its presentation of the story, ran a panel high up on the opening page headed Key Points. Here is the second of the three key points: "Wills is quoted as claiming "we killed all in sight"." There is no more reason to believe Tom Wills ever said those words than there is to believe he returned to the family home in Victoria and found his family's heads impaled on poles. The third Key Point repeats and compounds the fallacy: "He (Tom Wills) also described murdering an Aboriginal who stole his jacket".   Says who? The same anonymous author who implied Wills killed every Aboriginal person he met in later life.

The effect of the ABC's presentation of the story was to catapult Tom Wills into the binary universe branded with the words "we killed all in sight". If you don't believe me, type the words "we killed all in sight" into Twitter and see how many tweets appear using that quote to condemn Wills.

126

When I wrote my first book about Wills, *The Call*, in 1996, I didn't attempt to define him, instead presenting him as a series of possibilities. There was too much about him I didn't know to make a guess as to his true identity. When the book became a play at the Playbox Theatre, the first question one Indigenous cast member asked was, "Did Tom Wills go through men's business?" That is – was he initiated? I had to say I didn't know (although I doubt it). But he spoke the Tjapwurruing language, knew Tjapwurrung songs and dances, played their games, could use their weapons.

There are several ironies about the move from the Left to now "cancel" Wills. One is that if he's cancelled it will remove the only link between the Aboriginal game called marngrook and the game now called AFL. We'll be back at the idea that Australian football is a by-product of English school games. It was because he threatened that idea that he was attacked by individuals on the Right when my book, The Call, was published in 1996.

The people who most helped me write the book were descendants of Tom's brother Horace. It was Horace's grandson, Lawton Wills Cooke, then in his 90s, who told me his mother told him Tom played Aboriginal football as a kid growing up in Moyston. But the Wills Cooke family were divided in their view of the story. And, in my experience, the Queensland Wills descendants have a different view from their Victorian counterparts. The Victorian view was best expressed for me by Lawton Wills Cooke: "Poor old Tom, he wasn't much good unless he had a bat or a ball in his hand."

Queenslanders tend to see him as an individual thwarted by southern bureaucracy. One of the Queensland Wills told me with total assurance that he was the model for Tom Brown in *Tom Brown's School Days* (he wasn't).

To use film-maker Burns' phrase, Tom Wills is "tantalisingly complicated". In the immediate aftermath of the massacre, Wills' mother and sister cried out for deadly retribution. It is poignant, therefore, to consider that when he was passing through Geelong with the Aboriginal cricket team six years later he took them to meet his mother. There's a family document where his sister looks out the window and there they are.

Some people want Tom Wills to be a moral missionary. A Christ figure. I have always tried to temper that idea by talking about Ian Botham, the champion Somerset and England cricketer who walked out on Somerset after they sacked their two black West Indian players, Viv Richards and Joel Garner. No one sees Ian Botham as a moral missionary. No one thinks of him as a "progressive" because he's known to be a Tory. But he was also a sportsman and sport is a language and Ian Botham spoke the language of cricket big and loud and so did Garner and Richards. There was something between them that was not between Botham and the other players. It's in that's sort of way that sport transcends race.

I've also said that when Wills came back to Melbourne after the massacre and reprisal raids in Queensland, he was like a Vietnam veteran. Not all Vietnam veterans killed people during that war, but they knew that other Australian servicemen had and this shared consciousness was something they carried. And then they got back to Australia and found people thought they knew about the Vietnam war because it had been on the television news when in reality they knew next to nothing. I believe Wills faced similar psychological dilemmas.

Six years after the massacre, Wills was in western Victoria coaching the Aboriginal cricket team that became the first Australian cricket team to tour England. People have been asking ever since why he did. One possible explanation is religious. Rugby, when he went there, preached a creed called "muscular Christianity". Another is commercial – he was a professional sportsman and there weren't many paying gigs in the 1860s. Besides he knew he could do the job – he'd grown up with Aboriginal people. Also, in traditional Aboriginal culture, blaming Aboriginal people in Victoria for a murder committed by Aboriginal people in Queensland is as logical as blaming a Dane for a murder committed in Milan. That may have been Wills' attitude, too.

My guess – and, at some point with Tom Wills, we are all guessing – is that there was another attraction for him in being with the Aboriginal cricketers. Whatever their differences, there was one huge thing that Tom Wills had in common with his teammates – they had all lost family in the frontier violence. About 15 years ago, I was fortunate to meet the grandson of the member of that team, the one known as Dick-a-Dick. The grandson, an old man called Jack Kennedy, lived in Dimboola and took me to the ruins of the Ebenezer mission where Dick-a-Dick is buried. I asked Jack if he had heard stories about Tom Wills as a kid. He said he had, and added, "He died of the drink".

He didn't remember Wills badly. This also means that, at a time when Tom Wills was being remembered and talked about by Aboriginal people in western Victoria, he was not being remembered or spoken about in white society. He was cancelled in the 19th century because he committed suicide (by stabbing himself through the heart with a pair of scissors). He was buried in an unmarked grave. Ironically, his birth date was arbitrarily given as January 1, the same birth date attributed to Aboriginal people on death certificates at the time. I see Tom Wills as an Australian Hamlet, a young man trapped in an impossible history.

SBS, Keira Jenkins, October 12 2021

WARNING: This article discusses themes that may be distressing to some readers.

Gayiri Country is beautiful, in the way that only some of the most rural parts of Australia can be.

The dryness in the heat, in the ground, and the river banks are both delicate and concerning.

The Country is mountainous, paddocks stretch out below as we fly in - the only patches of green in a landscape of red and brown.

The heat is oppressive and the streets are quiet, possibly because we've arrived in town in the warmest part of the day. But it's also unsettling, especially considering the reason I'm here.

Over 160 years ago - at least 300 Gayiri people were murdered on this Country.

Shot. Driven off cliffs. Massacred indiscriminately.

I've travelled to Central Queensland after reports alleging cricket and AFL pioneer Tom Wills participated in these attacks on Aboriginal people, in retribution for a massacre of white people at his family's camp. What I found was this story holds so much weight for the locals and still triggers a range of emotions.

In 1861, 19 settlers were killed on Cullin-La-Ringo station in Springsure, Central Queensland.

The retaliation attacks on Gayiri are the lesser-known part of the story, but for local Elder Darryl Black, it's important that people know the whole history.

"I love this country here but you get this funny feeling when you come here, like something upset everybody here," he says.

I feel the same funny feeling I have felt since I got off the plane. It's like I can physically feel the sadness in my chest, the heaviness of this Country.

Uncle Darryl welcomes my camera operator and I to his Country and bathes us in sandalwood smoke for protection.

"When I get the smoke going, I want you to stand in the smoke and wash yourself like you are having a bath," he says.

He feels it's his mission to teach others the truth about what happened here.

"The Wills massacre was the biggest massacre of white people in Australia's history," he said.

"What people don't know is that after that they came and slaughtered our people, out of the seven tribes on Gayiri Country, they slaughtered five straight away.

"Most of our people were killed here on this Country."

There is a memorial to the 19 dead settlers at the site of the Cullin-la-Ringo massacre.

But nothing for the more than 300 Gayiri people massacred in response.

Even today the Country is unsettling, and its eerie calm brings my cameraman to tears.

I grew up listening to stories of massacres on my own Gamilaroi Country; my father, my grandparents speaking truth to our history.

Through my work, I've visited a number of massacre sites. I know the feeling, and it's something you never forget.

The recent allegations surrounding Tom Wills have frustrated Darryl, who says he's been trying to draw attention to these events for years.

But he adds, the history is not as clear cut as is being reported.

"Thomas Wills we always think he was a great man and was a great friend to the Aboriginal people so I wouldn't want to see his name distorted in any way like that," Uncle Darryl says.

The killings started over some sheep, which disappeared.

The local people were blamed - and Uncle Darryl says the Wills' neighbour Jesse Gregson shot a number of Aboriginal people.

Afterwards, he didn't ride straight home but went to the Wills' camp - leading the Aboriginal trackers, who had come for retribution, there.

"What happens then is the young bucks have been out hunting for the day and they come back to find their people have been shot... so they send out smoke signals to a neighbouring tribe over on Snake Range and they came over to track the people who killed their people," Uncle Darryl says.

"They followed the tracks and these tracks led them straight around to the Wills camp.

"The local mob pulled up and thought these can't be the people, we got along good with these people but the group they invited went straight in and slaughtered them straight away, in minutes, it was that quick and fast, from that, that's where the massacres started.

Historian and author Frank Uhr tells a similar story of the events that unfolded.

He believes the shepherds had fallen to sleep and their sheep had wandered off. To cover up their mistake they'd lied and said they were attacked by Aboriginal people and the sheep had been stolen.

"The local squatters, not Wills, organised a vigilante group," Mr Uhr says.

"They went and found the local clan, the nearest clan they could find, without thinking, without asking questions, without looking for the sheep, without understanding anything that went on, they just started shooting, they killed 20 people."

Frank said the attack on Cullin-La-Ringo following this killing was done "quietly, quickly and with utmost effect".

And the reprisals after that were "horrific".

"The local stations organised vigilante groups," he says.

"They started pushing the Aboriginals up into a mountain area or a hill area. As they were about to attack or be attacked by the Aboriginals coming back down the hill the native police came in and that was disastrous."

The base for these vigilante attacks - Rainworth Station, was owned by Wills' neighbour Gregson, he says.

"There's a famous stone fort on Rainworth station which was probably a storehouse of some sort, which they're fabled to have turned into a fort," Mr Uhr says.

"Gregson owned Rainworth at that stage and that became the base for the reprisals too."

The story is difficult, and, like many events of the time, there are multiple versions of what unfolded.

Uncle Darryl believes telling the truth about the history will lead to the eventual healing of his Country.

"I'd like to see a sorry day for our mobs here, white and black," Uncle Darryl tells me.

"We all sit down together, have a big sorry day, have a barbeque and we all come together and face each other and shake each other's hands".

The Tom Wills Picture Show

Martin Flanagan, journalist at the Age, has often written of the great Wonders of Australian Sport, his love of the AFL, of the importance of Aboriginal players in the highest echelons of Australian sport.

A few years ago he threw himself at the mysterious and distressed figure of Tom Wills - our early Colonial cricket celebrity, who put together the Aboriginal Cricket Team set for Great Britain in 1868 - and helped write the original Code for Australian Rules. A hero for several original clubs - Melbourne, Collingwood and Richmond for example. Yet things fall apart, as things have often done for our sporting stars...

So Flanagan went deeper: "I dared myself to actually picture Tom Wills in the various situations I knew him to have been in during his life and backed my fancy. It was like entering a creative delirium. Pictures appeared before me which I wrote down in scenes. If I do the same thing in ten years' time, I may come up with a different story but I doubt that will happen. I doubt the energy that accompanied the writing of this treatment will ever return."

And so we have his The Tom Wills Picture Show, shedding light on a most complex character...

Illustrated, published by ETT Imprint, Exile Bay.